Praise of The Formul

"The Formula for Financial Freedom is a ...
It captures the energy, enthusiasm and actual experience of the author. Doc Yadav came to America with almost nothing, started a business with almost nothing, developed a formula for success and achieved the American dream. He shares his formula in a step by step fashion which will serve the needs of the aspiring as well as experienced entrepreneurs to achieve success and happiness."

> — Steven R. Feldman, M.D., Ph.D., Author
> Compartments (compartmentsbook.com)

"The Formula for Financial Freedom offers a truly comprehensive look at starting one's own business and working one's way toward success. In addition to providing a tremendous amount of information in a relatively short space, the author adds plenty of personal stories and amusing anecdotes to make the book very readable. The book should serve as a valuable desktop reference and guide for business owners."

> — CreateSpace Editorial Comment

"Doc Yadav's accounting of his life through this book is truly an amazing entrepreneurial story which could only happen here in America. Dr. Yadav generously shares his formula and vision of success to everyone who reads this book."

> — Gigi Stauss-Dieckgraefe, President
> Rainforest Coastal Labs (rfclabs.com)

"The book is very effectively organized, taking entrepreneurs from A to Z---from how to tell if they have the right drive and mind-set to start their own business to how to plan an exit strategy and enjoy the fruits of their labors in retirement."

"The Formula for Financial Freedom is a great entrepreneur's handbook, bringing together in one easy-to-read and comprehensive publication all the basic but vital knowledge and advice on entrepreneurship. Plus, this book offers important "inside" information and "street smart" that Doc Yadav has gained through his years of running a successful business of his own."

— Daniel K. Tipton, Sr., Owner
Tipton Systems (tiptonsystem.com)

As the owner of a well-established small business, I found much of the information in *The Formula for Financial Freedom* helpful. Doc Yadav's perspective is unique, and he covers all aspects of small business ownership. It's a must read for anybody who wants to start, run or improve his/her business.

— John C. Hyde, President
Architectural sheet Metal Systems, Inc.
(architecturalstl.com)

THE FORMULA FOR FINANCIAL FREEDOM

How I Turned My $15 into Millions as an Entrepreneur

Kamal "Doc" Yadav, Ph.D.

Founder, Chemco Industries, Inc.

Formula Press

5731 Manchester Ave, St. Louis, MO 63110, USA

www.theformulaforfinancialfreedom.org

ISBN: 1450529011
ISBN-13: 9781450529013
LCCN: 2010906717

CONTENTS

convert American eagles into European pigs. An American success story.

INTRODUCTION

Why You Need this Book?

Many native-born Americans ask themselves, "Why am I still struggling financially when many immigrants come to the United States and get rich?"

I'm proud to say that I'm living the American dream.

I came to America in 1961 from a rural village in northeastern India between New Delhi and Calcutta. The son of a rice farmer, I'd known nothing but poverty and backbreaking labor my entire childhood.

The moment I arrived in America, I was rich…in dreams and determination.

I spoke broken English. I had $15 in my pocket.

Today…

I am the president and chief executive officer of Chemco Industries, Inc., a multimillion-dollar corporation that makes environmentally friendly cleaning products. I've been honored by the U.S. Small Business Administration and the Missouri House of Representatives as a champion of the free enterprise system. Chemco's customers range from the U.S. Army, Navy, Air Force, major industries and institutions to ordinary people cleaning their rugs.

I am writing these words from my study in the luxurious home built on the same grounds where Branch Rickey—the celebrated president of the St. Louis Cardinals and later the Brooklyn Dodgers—lived in his mansion. To this day I find it remarkable that I am living in such proximity to the man who signed the first African American to play Major League baseball—Jackie Robinson, another example of the American dream fulfilled.

I've come a long way from the water buffaloes and rice paddies of northeastern India. It has felt like a journey of a million miles from riding an elephant to driving a brand new Mercedes. As a result of the success that is Chemco, I'm a multimillionaire. My wife and I enjoy visiting Hawaii, London, Alaska, Paris, and other beautiful and exotic places. We just got back from our fabulous Christmas holiday vacation at Puerto Vallarta, Mexico and are looking forward to our next vacation trip to Vienna, Madrid, and Barcelona this spring. I am grateful for everything I've been able to achieve in this great country. Now I have a new American dream to help everybody achieve what I achieved—no matter where they live or where they come from. I am grieved to see our people—living in the wealthiest country of the world—go to bed hungry, become homeless, or live from paycheck to paycheck. It's not that they don't want to get out of their miserable conditions. They do, but they don't know how.

In India, there's a saying: When the student is ready, the teacher appears.

You are reading this book because you are ready. The lessons offered in this book are based on my ten-plus years of education as an undergraduate and graduate student at various educational institutions and over thirty-five years as an entrepreneur, all the while perfecting my formula for financial freedom.

I started my entrepreneurial life without any formal education in business—an advantage for learning real-life business skills. You don't have to have a Ph.D. degree or even a college education to be wealthy. If you have a burning desire to succeed, a good work ethic, and a willingness to learn and change, practicing the step-by-step formula described in this book will help you achieve your dream of financial independence.

I believe one reason many Americans don't succeed as entrepreneurs is because they go to business schools. There, professors teach them what they themselves learned in business school. So the students learn what's in the officially approved academic books but are unprepared for life in the real world. Business school prepares them to work for entrepreneurs and large corporations rather than for themselves.

It's great to learn what you can from books—I've read many business books myself. I've gone to many seminars and workshops. But I learned from writers who first were successful on their own, from Donald Trump to Jack Welch.

I'm here to teach you what works in real life—not what works in textbooks.

This book is your one comprehensive blueprint for succeeding as an entrepreneur and achieving your financial independence.

I will share with you the viewpoint I brought to America as an outsider from another culture. I will share the beliefs that supported my success and show you how you can use these beliefs to empower your own rise as an entrepreneur and realize the American dream. You can achieve happiness and wealth as an entrepreneur—even if you were born in America. You have many advantages over me, especially the stage I was when I started in this country. You just need to know how to maneuver the rigid financial, legal, and bureaucratic structures that are standing in your way as stumbling blocks. I show you how to turn these and other stumbling blocks into stepping stones. You will still be the quarterback of your game, but I will help clear the field for your touchdown.

It matters nothing to me whether you're an immigrant in America, as I was, whether you were born in America, or whether you live in another country—basic business principles apply everywhere and to everyone. America is the land of opportunity, but many people are getting rich all over the world, from India to Brazil. Many would-be entrepreneurs in the old Communist societies of the Soviet Union and Eastern Europe are eager to learn how to succeed in business. Even China, which is officially still a Communist country, is expanding its economy as rapidly as possible—encouraging everyone to think and act like an entrepreneur. Entrepreneurialism is spreading like wildfire everywhere. With the election of Nicolas Sarkozy as the president of France, reelection of Angela Merkel as the chancellor of Germany, and possible election of Conservative Party leaders in the United Kingdom in the next election cycle, the citizens of these countries are looking forward to a better life under the free enterprise system than what they have had under the centrally controlled economy of the past several years.

Although this is a joke, it could easily be a real story. A well-dressed chauffeur was driving the pragmatic premier of Communist China through Shanghai in a black Cadillac limousine. The city, which has recently seen the most remarkable building boom of its history, was bustling with activity. As he approached a T junction in the street, the chauffeur asked the premier whether he should take a left or a right. The astute, business-minded premier ordered, "Give the signal for the left turn but take the right." Throughout the developing countries of the world, hundreds of millions of people are pinning their hopes for achieving a better life on starting a business whether it's a sidewalk café, a vegetable stand, a coffee shop, a day care center, a private school, a toy factory or a high-tech manufacturing facility. They can benefit by the formula for business success explained in this book.

According to the Office of Advocacy of the U.S. Small Business Administration, there were 29.6 million businesses in the United States in 2008. Small businesses with fewer than 500 employees represent 99.9 percent of all businesses in our country. It's a sad fact that 50 percent of all new businesses fail within the first five years. Small firms with fewer than twenty employees spend 45 percent more time per employee annually than larger companies to comply with federal regulations. This excessive burden placed unfairly on small businesses does not include regulations that are passed by states, counties, cities and townships on a regular basis. If you are a small-business owner you will get the rubber-meets-the-road information from this book to exert your constitutional rights to fight against these heavy-handed bureaucrats, build a successful business against all odds, and achieve your financial freedom to enjoy the finer things of life.

Americans are celebrating entrepreneurialism more now than they have in many decades. The recession of 2008-09 has wiped out some of the giant, inefficient, too-big-to-succeed companies and paved the way for smart, well-informed and ambitious entrepreneurs to succeed beyond their imaginations. This is the opportunity of their lifetime.

As big corporations downsize and buy one another out, many Americans suddenly find themselves without jobs or are forced to take early retirement. We all know that job security is a thing of the past. Many of these suddenly unemployed people are now looking to strike out on their own as entrepreneurs. If you are one of them, this is a timely book for you.

Many people in the baby boom generation (persons born in the United States between January 1, 1946, and December 31, 1964) will soon be leaving their jobs, but they won't be spending their time sitting in a rocking chair or playing golf. They'll be using their golden years to start the businesses they've been dreaming about for years. If you are even thinking about starting a part-time or full-time business, in home or out-of-home enterprise, or a small or large corporation, you are holding in your hands the road map of your journey to success and happiness. Or, if you really want to take it easy and enjoy your retirement, this book has a whole chapter to show you how you can have a financially secure, happy, and fulfilling life in your retirement.

If you have the inner drive to succeed as an entrepreneur and a business owner, I want to help you by sharing what I have learned from thirty-five years of running a successful company, starting with a small amount of my own money and self-financing my growth and expansions.

I want to share with you the lessons I learned the hard way.

I cannot guarantee you success, but I can guide you to the right road and point you in the right direction with the rubber-meets-the-road information to achieve your financial freedom and life's true happiness as an entrepreneur and a business owner.

This book is your blueprint to wealth.

CHAPTER I

How to Find the Entrepreneurial Spirit within You

Waiting rooms in most doctors' offices are crowded, and patients wait and wait, in some cases for hours, before they are called into the examination room to be seen first by a nurse and eventually by the physician.

In 1966, just after receiving my Ph.D. in chemistry, I got a job as a chemist. My employer had very good medical and hospitalization coverage. Since I had not had a thorough physical checkup for several years, I called a general physician, who had been highly recommended to me, for an appointment. The doctor's receptionist, after checking the doctor's schedule, gave me an appointment at 2:00 P.M. two weeks later. I took that afternoon off from work and reached the doctor's office at 1:30 P.M. on the day of the appointment. I checked in with the receptionist. She gave me a form to fill out. Since I had only half an hour before my appointment, I filled the form out as quickly as I could and turned it in to the receptionist. She asked for my insurance card, copied it, returned it to me, and asked me to take a seat in the waiting room, which was crowded with other patients. At 2:00 P.M., the nurse came out, and I thought I would be invited in. But she called for another patient. Now it was 2:15 P.M., so I got up and knocked on the receptionist's window and asked her what was happening because my appointment was at 2:00 P.M. She answered in a very casual manner, "Please wait. You'll be called very soon." Soon it was 2:30 P.M., and I still had not been called.

Now I was getting frustrated. I talked to another patient sitting next to me about this undue delay. He said that most doctors booked more patients than they could handle in a timely fashion and that this type of delay was normal. While I was talking to my fellow patient, my name was called, and I followed the doctor's secretary to a small examination room. It was 2:45 P.M. I was asked to undress and wrap myself in a white cloth and wait. At 3:00 P.M., a nurse came in and took my temperature and blood pressure. The doctor did not come in until 3:30 P.M. He was very nice and professional, but he did not say a word about the long delay. I did not like this kind of elitism. In those days, most insurance companies wanted patients to pay the doctor bills and wait for reimbursement by the company. I received a bill for $450 for my visit and for various tests in the doctor's office. I sent a check for $350, with a note stating that I had deducted $100 for my time. I explained that since I did not work for the doctor, I could not wait for him. As a matter of fact, the doctor worked for me, so he should wait for me! I should not wait for someone I am paying. I got a call from the doctor's bookkeeper when she received my check. She told me that most patients did not mind waiting. I said, "I do," and I told her that I was going to send her a $100 check this time, but in the future, if I had to wait for more than ten minutes, my clock would run, and I would charge the doctor for my time as he does for his. The result? I went to that same doctor for the next twenty-six years, and I was always called in within ten minutes. Since then, I have had several new doctors and during my first visit, I explain to each of them very clearly that they work for me and all have respected my expectations.

Reading this anecdote might lead you to believe that I was being some sort of brat or arrogant. But in truth, I was being an entrepreneur. The first rule of being an entrepreneur is to know your rights and have the courage to defend them.

Who is an entrepreneur? *Merriam-Webster's* defines *entrepreneur* as someone who organizes and assumes the risk of a business or enterprise. Jeffrey A. Timmons developed one of the best definitions in his book *The Entrepreneurial Mind*. He wrote, "Entrepreneurship is a human, creative act that builds something of value from practically nothing. It is the pursuit of opportunity regardless of the resources at hand. It requires a vision and the passion and commitment to lead others in the pursuit of that vision. It also requires a willingness to take calculated risks."

There are three categories of entrepreneurs. They are:

1. *Innovative entrepreneurs.* They foresee and envision a clear need by the consumer and create a product or service to fill that need. In doing so, they help to create a new industry, which eventually may employ millions of people. They develop a new product or new idea and build a new business around their new concept. This entrepreneurship requires a substantial amount of creativity and ability to see social and consumer needs, patterns, and trends before they are evident to the pub-

lic. Innovative entrepreneurs include Thomas Edison, who, in addition to inventing incandescent lighting, was instrumental in the invention or discovery of the phonograph, motion pictures, the electric-traction motor, storage batteries, telephones, and the "Edison effect," the phenomenon that led to the invention of the vacuum tube and to radio and television. Each one of these is an industry in itself today. Besides Edison, other innovative entrepreneurs include William Hewlett and David Packard of Hewlett-Packard, Steven Jobs of Apple, and Bill Gates of Microsoft, just to name four of the most successful. They, and people like them, are true innovative entrepreneurs who had the vision, took the risks, developed the product, filled the need, and succeeded beyond their wildest dreams.

2. *Creative entrepreneurs.* They build a new business around an old idea, concept, or product. Perhaps most famously, Sam Walton built a giant retailing and distribution business—Walmart—around the old concept of Ben Franklin's nickel-and-dime business. Ray Kroc offered hamburgers and french fries through worldwide franchises—McDonald's—even though the idea of a hamburger stand was not new. W. Clement Stone of Combined Insurance Company of America built a giant sales force to sell low-premium life insurance door-to-door. Similarly, Mary Kay Ash built the multibillion-dollar Mary Kay cosmetics organization. Lee Iacocca saved Chrysler from bankruptcy and preserved thousands of jobs by being a creative entrepreneur.

Michael Bloomberg, founder of Bloomberg Business News and the current mayor of New York City, started his own wire service, competed against giants like Dow Jones, and succeeded through hard work and creative ways. He spent $120 million of his own money to win his third mayoral term and achieve his lifelong dream of occupying the mayor's office. Creative entrepreneurs bring their creative thinking, the latest technology, and superb management skills to provide the same old products and services in newly efficient and economical ways to the consumer.

3. *Sustaining entrepreneurs.* They buy an existing business and run it the same way it has always been run. For example, they purchase franchises and run them as the franchiser's training and policy manual recommends. These entrepreneurs have to run the day-to-day operation in their own imaginative ways and take financial risks like all entrepreneurs do. People who run restaurants, day care centers, private and vocational schools, hardware stores, independent bookstores, hotels/motels, and other retail, wholesale, or manufacturing businesses are all sustaining entrepreneurs. The majority of entrepreneurs belong to this category.

All entrepreneurs—whether they are innovative, creative, or sustaining—willingly assume responsibility for their success or failure. They follow their vision and make any sacrifices necessary to create success and happiness for themselves, their families, their employees, and their communities. Most, if not all, of them are *possibility thinkers*; in other words, they spend more time thinking about success, rewards, and profits than failures, punishments, and losses. They continuously strive to make things work for their venture, and if things don't work, they feel that they have to do better next time by using the experience of their failure. Thomas Edison, who failed over a thousand times before he invented the lightbulb, is an example of a superb possibility thinker. When Edison was asked about his failures, he replied, "I never failed. As a matter of fact, I succeeded in finding a thousand ways of how not to make a lightbulb."

I was born and raised in a small, dusty, poor village in India. When I was in the eighth grade, a science teacher showed me the magic of chemistry by changing the color of water with the addition of different chemicals. That experiment ignited what would prove a lifelong interest in chemistry. In 1959, I received my bachelor of science degree in chemistry with top honors from Bihar University in India. I taught chemistry there for two years and then enrolled at the University of Missouri in Columbia in the fall of 1961. There, I met a distinguished professor, Dr. George B. Garner, who became not only my academic adviser but also my lifelong friend and mentor. Under Dr. Garner's guidance, I received my master's and doctorate degrees, both in chemistry, in 1962 and 1966, respectively. After that, I worked in the chemical industry as a research and quality-control chemist and later as a chemical salesperson and sales manager. In 1975, my wife and I founded Chemco Industries, Inc., and our lives changed for the better in more ways than one. During the last thirty-five years, all our dreams have come true. We enjoy the real meaning of financial freedom in this land of the free and home of the brave. I strongly believe that if a person of my background, with a funny accent and awkward walk, coming to this land of opportunity with $15 in his pocket can make it, you can make it, too, if you so desire. While I cannot guarantee that all of you will reach the same level of success and happiness, I can promise you that if you study, follow, and practice the principles and concepts outlined in the following pages, you will have a better chance to succeed than I had when I started my business.

Based on my thirty-five-year practice of entrepreneurship and continuous study of various business books and writings, I have come to the conclusion that there are ten basic qualifications required to be a successful entrepreneur and business owner. Study each of the ten qualifications below and give yourself a grade on a scale of zero to ten, with ten being the best. With this test, you are both student and teacher. Being honest and practical in grading yourself is very important to your success.

QUALIFICATION #1

Do you have a burning desire to be financially independent?

We are blessed to live in the greatest country on earth, the United States of America. As of 2000, the total population of the world was 6 billion (6,000,000,000) people, out of which there were approximately 300 million (300,000,000) living in the United States. That means we Americans were only 5 percent of the world's population. In 2000, the world's total economy was $40 trillion ($40,000,000,000,000) and the American economy was over $10 trillion ($10,000,000,000,000). That means our economy was 25 percent of the world economy. In other words, 5 percent of the world's population was enjoying 25 percent of the world's wealth. During the last ten years, that disparity has grown even further. No wonder we are the envy of the world. People from all over the globe want to come here, and enjoy the prosperity and opportunity created by our free enterprise system.

During the summer of 1995, I was elected as a Missouri delegate to the White House Conference on Small Business. There were twenty-two hundred of us from all over the country in the nation's capital for a week, discussing the various challenges facing small businesses. I participated in one discussion group that considered the burdens levied on small businesses by the Occupational Safety and Health Administration, the Environmental Protection Agency, and the Internal Revenue Service. There were about two hundred delegates in that group, which was presided over by a businesswoman assisted by a parliamentarian and an official from the U.S. Labor Department. The discussion got very heated at one point, and many of us were talking at the same time about the problems facing us—unannounced inspections, undue citations, and outrageous fines. To maintain decorum, the chairwoman stood up and yelled, "Time out! Time out! Let me ask you a question. How many of you in this room are millionaires? Please raise your hands." Ninety percent of the delegates raised their hands. The chairwoman said with a grin, "I rest my case. Things are really bad out there."

According to Stanley and Danko, coauthors of The Millionaire Next Door, in 1996, approximately 3.5 million households in America (out of 100 million households) had a net worth of $1 million or more. That means, in 1996, 3.5 percent of American households included millionaires. Despite the recent economic downturn, that number has only grown over time.

In *The Millionaire Mind*, Thomas J. Stanley shows the percentage of millionaires in different occupations.

Business Owner – Entrepreneur	32 percent
Senior Corporate Executive	16 percent
Attorney	10 percent
Physician	9 percent
Others	33 percent

Without a doubt, as a business owner-entrepreneur, you can not only become a millionaire, but you can also help your employees, customers, and community. Do you have the desire and longing to be one of the next millionaires and enjoy the finer things in life? If you do, read on. Uncover what inspires you most as a business owner and entrepreneur. Do you want to have a large bank account and financial security? Do you want to live in your dream house? Do you want to drive a luxurious automobile? Do you want to travel to exotic places? Do you want to send your children to the best schools and colleges? Do you want to give to charity or build a hospital for the poor and needy? You succeed in what you are passionate about. Your passion connects you to your inner power that energizes you, your thoughts, words, and actions. Define your dream and open a world of wonderful possibilities. If you can dream it, you can do it. Your goal is your dream with a deadline on it. Once you set a date for when you want to turn your dream into reality, your dream becomes your goal. The self-imposed deadline helps you focus your mind and concentrate your efforts in turning your dreams into reality. Once you build your goal, your goal starts building you. Do you want to be a great person? Build your goals worthy of that great person you want to be, and the rest is history.

There is an abundance of wealth in this country. According to the 2000 Census, the following is the distribution of wealth among Americans:

Percentage of Population	Percent of Wealth Owned
1 percent	23 percent
5 percent	40 percent
10 percent	60 percent
20 percent	80 percent

If you still need some help in inspiring yourself to be a part of the 20 percent of the population that owns 80 percent of the wealth in this country, take note of what the most successful people in your community do for a living, in what kind of houses they live, what type of car they drive, where they vacation, and to which schools they send their children. Take a Sunday afternoon and visit their neighborhoods. If you get a chance, talk to them. Most successful people are very nice and open. By talking to them, you will find that most of them are not geniuses, but they do have a strong desire to succeed. By meeting them, you may develop the same desire. If they can do it, you can do it. Become involved in a charitable organization of your liking and be a good volunteer. Some successful people who can arouse your interest to be successful and even become one of your mentors may notice you. It is said that everything happens twice, once in your mind and then in your life. Napoleon Hill in his famous book *Think and Grow Rich* said, "Whatever the mind can conceive and believe, it can achieve."

QUALIFICATION #2

Do you believe in yourself and your abilities?

Entrepreneurs are highly self-confident individuals who have established high standards for themselves. They are hard driving, emotionally charged, and highly enthusiastic about what they are doing and what they are planning to do. Their confidence in their abilities breeds' success, and their success breeds further confidence in their abilities. Part of the entrepreneur's job is to stand out. But entrepreneurs will have a hard time doing that if they don't believe they are worthy of the spotlight.

If you lack self-confidence, you can develop it by visualizing all the successes you have had in sports, academics, extracurricular activities, social relationships, and business affairs in the past. Live and rejoice in those moments of success mentally. Remember how you felt when you were praised for success or had won a prize, trophy, award, certificate, or medal. Capture that moment and visualize it as often as possible, especially when things are not going your way. Do not think about the defeats, losses, or insults that you have endured. Concentrate only on the good things, on your successes, and on your strengths. Let the feelings of success soak in your being—body and mind—and enjoy every second of it. You will feel energized and powerful. Try it.

Read biographies of people you admire. Such books I have read include *How to Win Friends and Influence People* by Dale Carnegie, *Think and Grow Rich,* by Napoleon Hill, and *I Dare You* by William Danforth. There are many self-help books that you can get from your local library, free for the asking. Get a library card and dive into the ocean of knowledge with your total commitment to be the best, the most informed, and the most successful. Get audiocassettes and CDs and play them in your home or car. The ideas you will be exposed to can build your confidence and revolutionize your life. It is said that if you can use 10 percent of your abilities, you will be a genius. So it is not the lack of your abilities but the lack of their use that steals the confidence you should have in yourself. Think about it: if you do not believe in yourself, why should somebody else believe in you? If you are betting on horses, football games, the stock market, or buying a lottery ticket, you must believe that you are going to win. You have a five-million-times better chance of seeing John Madden in a True Value Hardware store than winning a $1 million lottery.

A few years ago, while paying for gas at a service station, a clerk said, "Doc, you should buy a lottery ticket." (My nickname is Doc. Most people had problems in pronouncing my first name, Kamal, sometimes calling me Camel or Kamil. One of my employees started calling me Doc. Since I am a *doctor* of chemistry, that nickname appeared to be appropriate and has stuck with me ever since.) "You could win millions." I replied, "I'm still working on my own million-dollar lottery and feel pretty close to winning it." I have not yet told her that I did win that million-dollar lottery—not by buying a lottery ticket but by being successful in my own business. What I am asking you to do is to bet on yourself, take a chance on yourself, and believe in yourself. Be your own million-dollar lottery and bet on a sure thing.

QUALIFICATION #3

Do you have skill, expertise, or experience in an actual business?

In this age of the twenty-four-hour media cycle of do-it-yourself programs and infomercials, a large number of people in our society know and talk about a lot of things. But when it comes to *doing those things*, they cannot or will not get them done. Knowing and talking about something does not give you a skill. Practicing what you know gives you a skill, and you need skill and expertise to succeed as an entrepreneur. I very often say, if talkers had been successful in business and made a lot of money, I would have had a tough competition. There are many talkers out there. Be a doer—not just a talker. If you have an idea for a business venture, get a job in that type of business, at any salary or even on commission. Learn from the inside how that business is run, who its customers are, how it gets them, how it keeps them, who its suppliers are, what its profit margins are, how much it pays, and how it keeps its employees. Once you go into your employer's business with an entrepreneurial mind, you will learn fast. You do not have to work there long. With the working knowledge of that business, you go out and start your own first business in a similar model. Your chances of success will be a lot higher than if you go into your business without that experience.

From the day I began my business, even before I started my business, I knew I wanted to manufacture and sell environmentally safe specialty cleaning products for industries and institutions. As a chemist, I knew how to make these products, but I did not know how to sell them. So I got a job as a commission salesman in a small company that sold specialty cleaning chemical products. I worked in that company for five months. During that short period, I learned how to sell and manage a sales force. With that brief experience, I started my business and succeeded from the very beginning because of that acquired skill. Remember, starting out, you don't have to be the very best in your industry—just better than average.

Perhaps you've heard the tale about the two men, John and Gary, who went fishing in the backwoods of the Northwest. The weather was humid, making for a lazy day along the banks of the river. Even the fish were lazy—they just weren't biting that day. The two friends were dozing when they heard rustling sounds in the nearby woods. John turned to see a grizzly bear coming toward them at a quick pace. Startled, he shook his friend. "Gary! Gary! Look behind you! A grizzly's coming at us, and she looks hungry!" Gary took one look at the bear reached for his rifle bag, but instead of pulling out his rifle, he pulled out his running shoes and started putting them on. John said, "Are you crazy? You can't outrun a grizzly." Gary turned to his friend, looked him in the eye, and said, "That's true, buddy, but I don't have to outrun the grizzly. I just have to outrun you." The moral of the story is that you do not have to be the best in the world to be successful in life and business.

QUALIFICATION #4

Are you willing to make sacrifices and take risks for your beliefs?

When my wife and I started Chemco Industries in May of 1975, we were not manufacturing our products. We were buying products under our name with a Chemco label and drop-shipping them as we got orders. I was on the road five days a week, calling on schools, hospitals, nursing homes, and municipal offices in small towns in Illinois and Missouri. I had learned from previous experience that there was less competition in small towns, and the people there were a lot nicer and more receptive to Chemco and me. I used to stay in small motels; most of them had old showers with only two settings—hot and cold. If you turned the knob right, it got cold; if you turned the knob left, it got hot. But for only $10 a night, you could not do any better, even though the value of $10 in 1975 was a lot more than it is today.

I used to get an early start at 7:00 A.M. calling on the street departments, township road commissioners, and courthouses where the maintenance engineers and housekeepers reported for work bright and early. I would catch them before they got busy in their daily work schedule. In spring and summer, at around 4:00 P.M., I would go to my motel, wash up, and get an early dinner if I was hungry. Then I would hit the road again and call on Veterans of Foreign Wars posts, American Legions, other service clubs, mayors, township road commissioners, and municipal swimming pool managers, sometimes even calling on them in their homes to discuss their cleaning chemical needs. When I visited them, I found that during these after-work hours, they were more relaxed and open to hearing me out. Every time I got turned down and failed to close a sale, my determination got stronger to make more calls and get more orders.

One day, I was working in a small town in southwestern Illinois. There was a big snowstorm, and six inches of snow covered the ground, making it difficult to get around. I had a choice: either check into a motel or find a way to sell my products. Talking to townspeople, I found out that most of the street department superintendents and township road commissioners and some other customers were hauling gravel from a nearby quarry. I drove to the quarry, found the manager, and established a rapport with him. I asked if I could use his desk for a few hours. He agreed since he was not using the desk at that time. I brought into his office my demo kit, products, and product catalogue, setting up shop at the manager's small corner table. Every time a customer arrived to pick up gravel, I asked the manager for the name of that customer. I would go out in the snow and ask the customer if he would come in, telling him I had something to show him. Instead of five hours spent staying warm and dry in my motel room and selling nothing, I managed to secure six sizable orders during that snowstorm. This experience of nurturing success from adversity proved to be an early turning point in putting me on the road to success.

Life is a do-it-yourself program. Ninety percent of your success depends on you and 10 percent depends on others and outside factors. So you have to continually learn, grow, and make sacrifices to make your business a success.

Once you decide to be a business owner and entrepreneur, you throw two things out—your watch and your ego. You do not get paid by the hour but by the results you obtain. You do not worry about what other people think of you. Concentrate on being more effective and more productive every day. Go after results with a vengeance. Stop pointing your finger toward others for your failures and shortcomings. When you point a finger toward others, look—at least three of your fingers are pointing toward you. Believe—really believe—that as the Rev. Robert Schuller said, "If it is to be, it is up to me."

QUALIFICATION #5

Do you have confidence in your idea and venture?

In the long run, the success of your business depends on the quality and usefulness of the product or service you provide to the consumer. Your confidence in your product or service should truly be beyond any question or doubt. Do you really believe your product or service will help your customer? Would you sell it to your mother, or, better yet, would you buy it yourself if somebody were trying to sell it to you? If your answer is yes, you are off to a good start and have the potential to succeed.

When we started Chemco, our product line consisted of environmentally safe cleaning, maintaining, and sanitizing chemical products for industries and institutions. We were so sure of the quality and effectiveness of our products that I told my customers, "If my products do not do what they are supposed to do, don't pay my bills. Call me at my toll-free number, and I will have them picked up at no charge to you. And if you did pay for them, your money will be refunded to you promptly." That no-questions-asked, 100 percent money-back guarantee resonated with my customers, and Chemco became the supplier of preference to large and small institutions throughout Illinois and Missouri. Since our humble beginnings in 1975, 90 percent of our business has been repeat business, and our satisfied customers have been purchasing from us year after year. One of the things of which I am most proud is that the very first customer I had on May 5, 1975, is still purchasing his products from us, thirty-five years later, without interruption.

QUALIFICATION #6

Can you lead others by your own example?

When you start your own business, you are appointing yourself leader and boss of your enterprise. The success or failure of your venture depends entirely on how well you handle this awesome responsibility. As a leader, you not only have to know your products and services well but also have to understand people well—your employees, customers, suppliers, and investors. You not only have to be a visionary, ready with your goals and plans, but also have to sell them to people who have, or could have, an interest in your products or services.

Since I am a chemist, I understood my products well, but for a long time I was not getting the sales success that I hoped for. Because of my science background, I concentrated on things more than people. To fill this void in my background, in 1975 I took a fourteen-week course, Effective Speaking and Human Relations, at the Dale Carnegie Institute of St. Louis. That's where I learned that 20 percent of business success is the result of product skills and 80 percent of the success is dependent on people skills. To be successful, you have to understand the principles of human behavior. In their book *Positive Thinking through Humaneering*, Cavett Robert and Merlyn Cundiff elaborate this principle in detail. For example, an engineer knows about an engine, so if your car engine is sputtering and making a lot of noise and you take it to an engineer—an auto mechanic—the mechanic will adjust the knobs so the air and the fuel mix right and your car runs smoothly. The same is true when you are working with human beings. Sometimes they are noisy, in a bad mood, and even ignorant of your thoughts and ideas. You have to be like the mechanic with your car. You have to understand a person's feelings, where he or she is coming from, and calm the person down so you can make your point of view clear. To be successful in business you have to be a human engineer, or what Robert and Cundiff call a *humaneer*.

As a leader, you cannot ask your subordinates to do any work that you are not willing to do yourself. You may, however, delegate some of your workload and responsibilities to your trained staff, which is a good way to expand your business. Even after delegating, you are responsible for your staff's actions. I do not suggest that you micromanage your staff, but remember, the buck stops with you. Delegation is an important part of leadership that must be learned. You must know what to delegate and what not to delegate. Four functions that you should never delegate are (1) your daily concentration on the sales of your products or services at a decent profit, (2) the collection of your accounts receivables, (3) doing what you yourself do best for your business, and (4) the proper investment of your profits. Functions that should be delegated to your staff include credit checks; manufacturing and quality control; delivery of products or performance of services; prompt billing and collection; and payment of bills, salaries, commissions, and taxes. After delegating, keep your staff motivated to perform their assigned duties with pride and accuracy. Trust them but periodically verify that they are doing their assignments as you have envisioned. The first rule of management is you inspect what you expect.

I want to emphasize that the sale of your products or services is the only activity of your business that contributes to your profit. All other activities—such as manufacturing, engineering, and advertising—contribute only to expenses. So you have to concentrate on achieving sales and profit to succeed.

Profitable sales will take care of a lot of obstacles and problems your business will face.

QUALIFICATION #7

Do you have effective communication skills?

Successful entrepreneurs are those who communicate effectively, and generate enthusiasm and confidence in others because they believe so deeply in themselves, their cause, and their vision. However, they understand that their own employees may not have the same commitment and therefore must be patiently nurtured, trained, and motivated to see the founder's vision and understand how they can also benefit from the success of the enterprise. Sam Walton of Walmart, John Chambers of Cisco, and Jack Welch of General Electric are examples of the master communicators of our time. While most entrepreneurs generally have big egos (something that is essential for turning stumbling blocks into stepping stones) they also must show humility in handling the needs of others as well as inquiries by investors, the public, and the media.

You have to sell your ideas and vision at all times to your customers. You have two types of customers—internal and external. Your employees, suppliers, bankers, investors, attorneys, and accountants are your internal customers. Your buying customers and clients are your external customers. You need to communicate with both types of clients in good times and bad. While communicating with your internal or external customers, always be positive and talk about how the success of your venture will help them realize their own dreams and goals, how your business is unique and different in serving your customers, and why you will be a big business someday.

Bad times can occur. Periods of recession and inflation are natural phenomena of the business cycle. They act as cleansing processes to eliminate the weaklings and create better opportunity for the well-managed and customer-focused operations. You have to stay calm, cool, and collected under trying circumstances. You are the captain of the ship. You are carrying a heavy and important load. Your ship is sailing in uncharted waters. You cannot afford to get discouraged or, worse yet, show your discouragement if your ship hits some rough seas. You have to steer your ship steadily to the shore of victory. I am sure that, through constant practice and patience, you will be up to it. Just remember, when the tide comes in, all boats rise. So will your business. Stay steady and confident. Good times always follow bad times, as day follows night.

QUALIFICATION #8

Are you a decision maker?

Ask yourself this question: "Do I make a decision on the basis of all the facts available to me at the present time, or do I wait and wait, thinking and brooding over the risk of making the wrong decision?" As an entrepreneur, you are pretty much on your own. You do not have the luxury of a large research staff or a bevy of consultants, advisers, and other executives. You are the general, and you are the army. In the entrepreneurial world, you have to make fast decisions, turn on a dime, and make a quick and sometimes risky decision to act on and capture the trend of the market, solve the customer's problem, and go with the flow of the time. If you are sitting on the fence, and you don't know which side to land on, with each tick of the clock you are losing time and opportunity. After a while, it would not make a difference which side of the fence you landed on. While you are sitting on the fence, in the agony of indecision, you are miserable. You have to believe that even a wrong decision is better than no decision. Making fast decisions helps you in two ways. If you make the wrong decision, you have enough time to correct the mistake. If you make the right decision, you and your business prosper and you have more time to enjoy the prosperity.

You do not know whether you have made a right or wrong decision until you act upon it and see the results. As an entrepreneur, you must have or be willing to acquire the *action habit*. No matter how many facts and how much information you have, or how much thinking and planning you have done, it is impossible to project right solutions to most day-to-day problems. Planning is a vital first step for getting results, but it can never substitute for action. In the final analysis, you have to make a decision to act and be ready to accept the consequences, whatever they may be. If you make a decision based on the facts available at the time and come out wrong, chalk it up as experience and move on. Peter Drucker, the management guru, once said, "Whenever you see a successful business, someone once made a courageous decision."

During the late 1970s and early 1980s, I heard that a lot of business people—doctors, lawyers, accountants, and others—with extra money were investing in real estate. I investigated and found out that the federal tax laws were extremely favorable to real estate investors. In those days, if your rental income was less than the bank loan payment and all other expenses—such as taxes, insurance, and repairs—you could deduct 100 percent of the loss from your salary and other income, which reduced your tax obligations to a lower rate and lower amount. In addition, you could take a depreciation expense on the property over a fifteen-year period, while the value of the same property was going up because of rampant inflation. It was very easy to get a bank loan. I bought a doctor's building, made some cosmetic improvements, and sold it eight months later, making over $150,000.

In those days, you had to reinvest that gain within a year in another real estate property to avoid high capital gains tax. So I bought more and more property. At one point, my real estate properties were appraised at about $4 million. Since I had started my real estate investment with $50,000 of my own money, I felt very proud of myself. Soon enough, that pride had a precipitous fall. During the Reagan presidency, the real estate laws were changed. After 1986, I could not deduct most of my real estate losses from my income. Losses were piling up in a hurry, and banks were getting uneasy, to say the least. A lot of savings and loan associations were investigated, and most of them went bankrupt. What do you do when your decisions are proved to be wrong because the facts that you based your decisions on had changed? Here is what my wife and I did.

At first, we tried to sell those real estate properties at a price as low as the balance of the loan we had on them. That meant we were willing to lose the equity we had built over a period of years. No matter how hard we tried to sell them, there were no takers. Since we were stuck with those properties, we decided to make the best of them. My wife started making improvements and raising rents. She managed the properties by herself. It took over five years to break even, and then our holdings became profitable. During the late 1990s, we sold them and made a huge profit. Even though my decision proved to be wrong, I had enough time to correct my mistake and come out a winner. Theodore Roosevelt wrote, "In any moment of decision, the best thing you can do is the right thing, the next best thing is the wrong thing, and the worst thing you can do is nothing."

If you read the biographies of successful and famous people, you will find that the path to greatness is always paved with mistakes and wrong decisions. But despite these mistakes, they made one right decision—to persevere through adversity to success.

QUALIFICATION #9

Do you have the stamina and determination to persist?

Running a small business is like barbecuing on an open fire. Sometimes, a sudden wind will make the fire stronger than you can control at the time. So you have to sprinkle some water to cool it down to the right level. But when the wind has passed, it will slow down more than you need for your cooking. Now you have to put some lighter fluid on it to build it back up. So is the life of a small businessperson.

There is never a dull moment in an entrepreneur's life. If you have a strong determination and you feel you are accomplishing something, you will not get tired of working long hours. You have to have energy and stamina to act like a thermostat not like a thermometer, and raise or lower the temperature as needed. Most people are like a thermometer. They just react to the rising or falling temperatures. They don't know what to do when things don't go their way and feel helpless. They are happy when things are good and depressed when things are bad. As an entrepreneur, you do not have that luxury. As the leader and head of your enterprise you are the thermostat. You have to take an immediate action and correct the situation as fast as you can to protect your business and prosper.

For the first five years of my business, I used to be on the road, working at least twelve hours a day, driving hundreds of miles to call on my customers in distant cities and towns. Then I would process orders and pay bills on the weekends. But I never treated it like work because I was coming closer to my goal of being financially independent. I say being in my own business I work only half days. I do not know which half of twenty-four hours I work. For an entrepreneur, a half-day's work means twelve or more hours of work every day.

I want to talk to you about *persistence*. It is said that the big shot of today was a little shot that kept shooting. Do you remember when you were learning how to ride a bicycle? Was it a smooth ride? If you are like most of us, you fell down. If you had never gotten back on the bicycle, you would have never learned how to ride it. What is true for learning how to ride a bicycle is true for learning how to run your business. You have to have persistence to win. I agree with Calvin Coolidge, who said, "Press on. Nothing in the world can take the place of persistence. Talent will not; nothing is more common than unsuccessful men with talent. Genius will not; unrewarded genius is almost a proverb. Education alone will not; the world is full of educated derelicts. Persistence and determination alone are omnipotent."

The basis of persistence is the power of your will. Lack of willpower is one of the major causes of failure in business and failure in life. Always remember: Winners never quit and quitters never win.

Willpower is built on the foundation of your true desire. If you have the burning desire to reach your life's mission, you will persist. You will endure the punishment that is involved in achieving anything of great value. You may have to change your strategy and adjust your plans and actions to meet the changing circumstances, but you won't have to change your goal as you are moving forward. Vince Lombardi said, "The difference between a successful person and others is not a lack of strength, not a lack of knowledge, but rather a lack of will."

Before 1985, a majority of Chemco's products were sold to municipal departments, sewer plants, water plants, street departments, fire departments, ambulance districts, township road districts, and county highway departments in rural areas. For their funding, these agencies were dependent on a federal program called *revenue sharing*, which financed most municipalities. In 1985, Congress passed a bill that President Reagan signed into law that discontinued revenue sharing. The consequences of that law were drastically negative for my business. I quickly realized that my customers still had facilities, buildings, equipment, and grounds to clean, sanitize, and maintain but not enough money to buy the supplies to do so. My sales dropped significantly. I had to make a decision to move and train my sales force from rural areas to large cities, where they had to learn new ways of doing business. These were painful years, but we persisted, and now over 60 percent of our business is in large cities. Our persistence paid off for us dramatically.

Hang in there. Give yourself time and room to maneuver around the situation. Something has got to give. If you do not, your adverse situation will. Rev. Robert Schuller so aptly put it, "Tough times never last; tough people do."

QUALIFICATION #10

Do you have a winning attitude?

Successful entrepreneurs have a winning attitude and the state of mind that, from the beginning, in all that they do, they are going to come out on top. When they engage their customers, their lawyer, their accountant, their banker, their investors, and their stockholders, they approach them as a winner, with a positive mental attitude. Personal qualities and attitude are the bedrock on which any business success is based. The mental ability to operate effectively in specific and challenging situations in the world of commerce is what ultimately makes or breaks an enterprise. To accomplish great things, a person must have the attitude that anything is possible and find how to make success a reality by creative and positive hard work.

Your attitude is the reaction inside of you to what happens outside of you. What happens to you happens to everybody. When it rains in your town, it rains on all the roofs. Once, years ago, I was driving on a St. Louis street where August Busch, then the president of Anheuser-Busch, had his multimillion-dollar mansion. There was a big snowstorm in St. Louis that week, and I observed that there was snow on the roofs of hundred-thousand-dollar homes. As I drove farther, as incredible as it may sound, there was snow even on the roof of the Busch mansion. As a matter of fact, there was more snow on his mansion than on the hundred-thousand-dollar homes. The point? Your capability to succeed is proportional to the challenges you tackle. You become a bigger entrepreneur if you can handle and withstand the burden of bigger problems. The following poem by Charles Swindoll may help you to attain the right attitude to succeed:

The longer I live, the more I realize the impact of attitude on life.
Attitude, to me, is more important than facts.
It is more important than the past, than education, than money, than circumstances, than failures, than what other people think or say or do.
It is more important than appearance, giftedness or skill.
It will make or break a company…a church…a home.
We cannot change our past…
We cannot change the fact that people will act in a certain way.

We cannot change the inevitable.

The only thing we can do is play on the one string we have,
And that is our attitude
I am convinced that life is 10 percent what happens to me
and
90 percent how I react to it. And so it is with you...

The Rev. Norman Vincent Peale, in his book *The Power of Positive Thinking,* said, "Any fact facing us is not as important as our attitude towards it, for that determines our success or failure."

In summary, here is the list of the ten characteristics needed to be a successful entrepreneur. Please grade yourself on a scale of one to ten, with ten being the best:

CHARACTERISTICS	POINTS									
	1	2	3	4	5	6	7	8	9	10
1. Do you have a burning desire to be financially independent?										
2. Do you believe in yourself and your abilities?										
3. Do you have skills experience or experience in an actual business?										
4. Are you willing to make sacrifices and take risks for your beliefs?										
5. Do you have confidence in your idea or venture?										
6. Can you lead by your own example?										
7. Do you have effective communication skills?										
8. Are you a decision maker?										
9. Do you have the stamina and determination to persist?										
10. Do you have a winning attitude?										
TOTAL:										
GRAND TOTAL:	_____ Points									

It is necessary to have a profound understanding of who you are and where you want to go. What are your deepest and greatest yearnings? Your ambition and winning attitude will keep you going, even when everyone else is ready to quit and close up shop. Some people seem to possess from their birth an almost compulsive desire to occupy the top spot. Others acquire it while growing up, perhaps from something they heard, something they read, something they observed, or somebody they met. No matter how you get this inner drive, one thing is sure: you have to have it to succeed.

As discussed earlier in this chapter, on a scale of one to ten, with ten being the best, grade yourself on these qualifications. Be honest, be realistic, and be objective. If your total evaluation is less than seventy, you may not be ready to be on your own. It is not that you are not entrepreneurial material, but that you need to study these qualifications and what they mean to you. Realize that the bend in the road does not mean the end of the road. Most successful people work harder on themselves than on the job they do. Working on improving yourself means reading more, listening more, observing more, and learning more. Before you earn, you have to learn. Learn more about your product or service. Learn more about your market and the quantity and quality of people who can purchase your product or service. Get more experience by working with someone who has been running a similar business and has been successful at it. But mostly learn more about yourself. Have patience and keep working toward your goal on a daily basis. You will know when you are ready. I hope that you will be the person you want to be. Everything else will follow. Your dreams of being a successful entrepreneur can come true.

If you gave yourself more than seventy points, I want to congratulate you. You are ready to take the plunge into the vast ocean of entrepreneurship and unlimited wealth. This book is a proven road map for your success and happiness. Good luck!

CHAPTER II

How to Structure Your Enterprise

Choosing the proper legal structure for your business is one of the most important decisions you will make. While it may not have much impact on the day-to-day operations of your business, it can have a huge impact come tax time, when you want to borrow money or attract investors, or in the unfortunate event you get taken to court. While it is possible to change your structure at a later date, it can be a difficult and expensive process. So it is advisable to make the right decisions the first time. There are five common legal structures that you can choose from. They are as follows:

Sole proprietorship

The sole proprietorship is a business that is owned by one person. To establish a sole proprietorship, all you have to do is obtain whatever business license may be required in your city or county. It is the simplest legal structure for a business; more than 75 percent of all businesses in the

United States today are sole proprietorships. The owner represents the company legally and fully.

Advantages of a sole proprietorship

- *Total control.* Since you are the sole owner, you run your business as you please. You can respond to your customers' needs quickly.
- *Reduced expense.* You have a minimal legal requirement. You can set up a sole proprietorship without an attorney, so it is less expensive than any other business setup. You visit the city or county clerk, fill out a simple form, pay the license fee, and get a retail sales tax number. You are in business the same day. It's as simple as that. With a sole proprietorship, you keep all the profits, which are your personal income.
- *Fast and easy tax filing.* As a sole proprietor, filing your income tax return is a lot easier than it would be if your business were a corporation. Simply file an individual income tax return (IRS Form 1040) including your business profits and losses. Your individual and business incomes are considered the same, and self-employed tax implications apply.
- *Bookkeeping is simple.* Handling cash, income, and expenses is a lot easier than with other business structures. No payroll setup is required to pay you. To keep things in order, establish separate bank accounts for your business and your personal finances.

Disadvantages of a sole proprietorship

- *Unlimited liability.* You are personally responsible for all liabilities. If you are engaged in litigation, whether for negligence or in a contract dispute, court judgments can claim all your personal assets because your personal wealth and assets are linked to your business.

- *Difficulties in raising capital.* Potential lenders see the sole proprietorship as a one-person operation and feel the risk is a lot greater with this business organization than with any other.

Partnership

A partnership is an association of two or more persons carrying on the same trade or business together. Each partner contributes money, property, labor, and personal skill, and each will share in the profits and losses.

Advantages of a partnership

- *Two heads are better than one.* You have the advantage of being able to draw on the skills and abilities of each partner and can complement each other.
- *Red tape is minimal.* Starting a partnership is relatively easy; however, it can be more complicated than a sole proprietorship because you have to find the right partner and draw up a partnership agreement.
- *High-caliber employees can be made partners.* You can attract and retain high-caliber employees by offering them the opportunity to become partners.
- *Partners pay only personal income tax.* The total income of the business is considered to be the personal income of the partners. This means there is no separate business income tax to pay.

Disadvantages of a partnership

- *Unlimited liability.* Like sole proprietorships, partners are responsible for all debts and legal judgments against their business.
- *Disagreement.* Disputes among partners can destroy the partnership, so initial foresight and preplanning in drawing up the partnership agreement can pay off later. Disagreements between or among partners are the major cause of partnership failures. For this reason, I do not recommend setting up a business as a partnership. As you know, 50 percent of all marriages in this country fail; marriages have love and sex to hold partners together but business partnerships don't.
- *Limited to the life of the business.* As with a sole proprietorship, the life of a partnership is limited. In case of the disability or death of a partner, the partnership is dissolved. Any time a new partner is admitted, dissolution of the old partnership and formation of a new partnership is mandatory.

Corporation

Unlike a sole proprietorship or a partnership, a corporation is a legal entity separate and distinct from its owner. Since a corporation is a separate entity, it can sue and be sued, own property, agree to contracts, and engage in business transactions. It is not dissolved with every change in ownership. The result of this legal framework is that corporations have the potential for unlimited life. To form a corporation, you must be granted a charter by the state, and it is recommended you have an attorney to incorporate.

Advantages of a corporation

- *Limited liability.* As a corporation, your liability is limited to the amount of your investment in the business. The creditors of the corporation cannot touch your personal assets.
- *Additional human resources.* Because of the separation of ownership and management, the corporate form of business can utilize the services of specialists such as attorneys, accountants, and consultants. A board of directors is required for a corporation, and a well-recruited board can be of great assistance in increasing the business's productivity, efficiency, and growth.

Disadvantages of a corporation

- *Double taxation.* Income that you draw from the corporation and the profit the corporation makes are taxed separately. This is the primary drawback to the corporate form.
- *Close regulation.* Numerous state and federal reports must be filed regularly since the government regulates corporations much more closely than it does any other form of business.

I feel that all small businesses sooner or later should incorporate. But in order to do so, you must have a strong and profitable operation going, or you will have to personally guarantee any and all liabilities and you lose the benefits of incorporating. However, this form will protect your personal assets from creditors should something happen to your corporation. In addition, a corporation offers you the opportunity of having tax-free medical, pension, profit sharing, and insurance plans as well as a safe-deposit box that your heirs can open upon your death without having an estate tax official present. While personal safe-deposit boxes are sealed on the death of the owner, corporation boxes are not because corporations do not die until bankruptcy. These corporate offerings are not designed to cheat on taxation but to take advantage of existing laws.

Subchapter S-corporation

An S-corporation is a separate legal entity; the corporation's finances and records are established and maintained separately and distinctly from the finances and records of the shareholders. Since January 1, 1997, an S- corporation can have up to seventy-five shareholders.

Advantages of a subchapter S-corporation
- *No double taxation.* The shareholders of an S-corporation are taxed directly, and the corporation itself is exempt from federal taxes. This is the biggest advantage of an S-corporation.

Disadvantages of subchapter S-corporation
- *Limited number of shareholders.* An S-corporation is limited to seventy-five shareholders.

Limited Liability Corporation (LLC)

An LLC has the daily activities of a partnership with the limited liability of a corporation. The owners of an LLC are called *members* rather than partners or shareholders. Since most states do not restrict ownership of LLCs, members may include individuals, corporations, other LLCs, and foreign entities. There is no maximum number of members. Most states also permit *single-member* LLCs, which are those having only one member.

An LLC is not a separate entity like a corporation or S-corporation. All the profits and losses of the LLC pass through the business to the LLC members, who report this information on their personal tax returns.

Advantages of an LLC
- It is much easier and typically less costly to form an LLC than it is to form most other types of business.
- The LLC itself does not pay federal income taxes.
- Members of an LLC are afforded limited liability.

Disadvantages of an LLC
- Members are subject to self-employment tax.
- This is a new form of business and not well understood.
- It is harder to raise money for an LLC than for a C- or S-corporation.

As you can see, there are many choices and factors to consider in setting up a business. Educate yourself and consider all your options carefully before taking the plunge in setting up your enterprise and finding out what legal structure are right for you and your business. Consult an accountant and lawyer who specialize in small business, particularly in businesses like yours.

Government regulations

Once you decide on a form for your business, you need to apply for and receive various permits from local, state, and federal regulatory agencies. They cover the following:

Local regulations

Local regulations pertaining to businesses are primarily concerned with taxation, public health and safety, and zoning. Although each community is different, the most typical forms are (1) business taxes and permits, (2) fictitious-name registration, (3) zoning restrictions, and (4) other regulations.

Business taxes and permits. Commonly referred to as a business license, this is a permit issued by the city or county in which your business is located. The fee for a business license is minimal and is based on your anticipated or actual annual gross sales; the license is usually valid for one or two years. Call your city or county clerk for details.

Fictitious-name registration. If you are planning your business under a name other than your own, you need to: (a) file the fictitious-name statement with the county clerk and (b) have the statement published in a newspaper of general circulation. As a convenience to their customers, most newspapers keep fictitious-business-name forms on hand and file the completed statements for you. The cost of filing and publishing should be less than $100.

Zoning restrictions. Each city in a county has a planning and zoning department, which creates a zoning plan to locate different businesses in different areas, such as retailing, wholesaling, distributing, and manufacturing. To find out the zoning restrictions for your business in your community, contact your local planning and zoning department or commission, located in your city hall or county courthouse.

Other regulations. Depending on the nature of your business, other local regulations may apply. For instance, if you are engaged in the preparation, processing, or serving of food products, you should contact your county health department. If you are manufacturing any product, contact your fire department. If you are engaged in retailing, contact your police department. By notifying these contacts, you will avoid lots of headaches in advance.

State regulations

State regulations may vary from state to state, but they include the following:

- *Seller's permit.* This permit (a) exempts you from paying sales tax on raw materials for manufacturing your products or merchandise you purchase for resale and (b) authorizes you to collect sales tax from your customers. To find out more about the permit, call your state retail sales license office.

- *Occupational license.* To set and maintain performance standards and protect consumers, most states regulate entry into specific occupations or professions like medicine, accounting, law, real estate, and cosmetology, just to name a few. If your business is in a regulated field, you should contact the state licensing board governing your occupation.

Federal regulations

- *Seller's permit.* This permit (a) exempts you from paying sales tax on raw materials for manufacturing your products or merchandise you purchase for resale and (b) authorizes you to collect sales tax from your customers. To find out more about the permit, call your state retail sales license office.

- *Occupational license.* To set and maintain performance standards and protect consumers, most states regulate entry into specific occupations or professions like medicine, accounting, law, real estate, and cosmetology, just to name a few. If your business is in a regulated field, y*Federal Employer Identification Number (FEIN).* If you employ one or more people in your business, you are required to have an employer identification number. This enables the government to verify that you are paying all necessary taxes, withholding the appropriate amounts from your employee's paychecks, and depositing the amounts on time. The number is simple to get and it is free. Just call the IRS and ask for an SS-4 form. Complete it and mail it to the Internal Revenue Service. You should receive the number within a couple of weeks.

- *Consumer protection regulation.* In order to protect the rights of the consumer, the federal government has established several commissions and boards, such as the Federal Trade Commission, the Interstate Commerce Commission, the Food and Drug Administration, and the Securities and Exchange Commission. To familiarize yourself with regulations that may apply to your business, write to the Federal Trade Commission, Washington DC 20580.

- *Trademarks, patents, and copyrights.* In addition to protecting the rights of consumers, the federal government also protects the rights of businesses and entrepreneurs as follows:

- *Trademark.* Although a business is not required by law to register its trademark—its name, symbol, device, or combination of these—it is advisable to do so. Your right to use your registered trademark extends for a period of ten years. For more information, write to the Patent and Trademark Office, United States Dept. of Commerce, Washington, DC 20231.

- *Patents.* If you develop a unique product, process, or design, it is advisable to obtain a patent, which will protect your exclusive right to use your invention for up to seventeen years. In this case, you should use a qualified patent attorney. The total cost may run from $5,000 to $10,000.

- *Copyrights.* A copyright protects the right of an individual to keep others from copying his or her creations. Obtaining a copyright is simple. To obtain the appropriate copyright form, write to the Copyright Office, Library of Congress, Washington, D.C. Complete the form and return it with the applicable fee, which is around $20.

In addition to the above government requirements and regulations, many businesses are also required to obtain permits that generally regulate the safety and appearance of an establishment—such as building and occupancy permits, and health permits if you are preparing food—all as defined local and/or state laws. Be sure that all the ducks are in a row with the various permits before you start your operation.

Your corporate attorney or accountant should be of help in this area. He or she generally has templates of the permits, and so such expertise should not be too expensive.

CHAPTER III

How to Finance Your Enterprise

Small businesses, especially start-ups have a variety of problems in finding the right source of financing. Your quest for your start-up capital requires the same level of attention, energy, and imagination as you have applied in finding your unique product or service. This chapter describes fourteen ways to finance your business. You decide which ones are available to and right for you.

Self-financing

Self-financing, which is also called bootstrap financing, is a direct investment of your own money. You make a loan to your business at a reasonable interest rate. In this way, you have provided the needed capital, with interest payments to you and the business deduction (the interest) for the corporation. This is the fastest way to get your business going. Since your own money is at stake, you will work harder to make your business a success. When I started Chemco in 1975,

I put up $5,000 of my own money to get started. Mary Kay Ash of Mary Kay Cosmetics did the same and built a multibillion-dollar business. If you believe in your business, put up your own money and get going rather than wasting your time and energy filling out loan applications and waiting for loan committees to meet. Go out and get some sales, get some customers, and see the adrenaline flowing in your veins and in your enterprise. You do not need a large office, office building, manufacturing plant, most modern office machines, or a large office staff when you are starting up. Your business starts with an order for your products or services. Even a small start is better than no start at all. Bootstrap financing is a way to pull you up without the help of others.

Trade credit

Being a chemist, I was inclined, even tempted, to manufacture my own products when I started my business. But I did not. I had a manufacturer private-label my products, then I went out and sold them at a good profit. Since my company did not have established credit, I had to deposit $2,000 with this manufacturer out of my $5,000 start-up capital. Every week, I would mail my orders in, and the manufacturers would drop-ship the orders to my customers, showing Chemco as the shipper; they would charge my account for their cost. I would bill my customers every week for the products shipped to them by my manufacturer. My wife and I were surprised when we started getting payments from our customers after just two weeks. Our bank account started growing every week. After that we started sending a check to our manufacturer for the products they had shipped for us. After six months or so, this manufacturer extended a line of credit to me. I used that manufacturer as my credit reference to establish my trade credit with other manufacturers and suppliers, and the rest, as they say, is history. *Trade credit* is an arrangement to buy goods or services without making advance cash payment.

I started my business with my own $5,000, but you will be surprised to know that I did not use all of it. I was operating from my home, and my overhead was extremely low, and profits were high. Within less than three years, I had saved enough to put a $50,000 down payment on a 13,000-square-foot office, warehouse, and manufacture building that I bought for $250,000. Slowly, I started formulating and manufacturing our top-selling products. Now we manufacture more than 70 percent of all the products we sell. We have formulated over three hundred products, as our customers needed them. I am most proud of the fact that all of our business expansion during the last thirty-five years has been self-financed.

I am blowing my own horn not to impress you with what I have done, but to tell you that you, too, can be successful starting with your own small amount of capital. It does not matter how small you start; it matters that you start and get going.

Even if you have $100, you can buy a secondhand bike and start a paper delivery route. Many mail-order businesses have been started with an initial capital of $100 and become a multimillion-dollar enterprise. Manufacturing companies can be started with a $1,000 initial investment. Many Internet companies have been started with a very small amount of capital, and some of them became giants like eBay. Often, latter-day behemoths had humble beginnings in a basement (IBM), garage (HP), or a warehouse (Walmart). Do not compare your situation with where they are today; compare your situation to when they first started out. Of all big businesses that you see today, many were tiny when they started.

Life insurance loans

If you own a life insurance policy that has built up cash value over the years, you can apply and be approved for a loan from your insurance company within a few days. One benefit of this is that the interest rate is low. You can pay the loan back any time and any way you are able to in order to restore the original cash value. However, if you cannot pay it back, in full or in part, your beneficiaries will have that much less to draw.

Home equity loan

You can borrow up to 80 percent of the equity you have in your home. Your equity is the appraised value of your house minus the mortgage you have on it. Since your home equity loan is secured by your home, you could lose your home if you do not repay your loan on time. The interest paid on the home equity loan is generally tax deductible.

Borrowing from your retirement plan

You can borrow up to 50 percent of your vested amount in your retirement, profit sharing or 401(k) plan. However, you cannot borrow from your IRA (except Roth IRA) or Keough accounts. You are not taxed on borrowed money if your loan meets tax law requirements.

Brokerage margin accounts

You can borrow usually up to 50 percent of the total value of the stocks and up to 90 percent of the government securities like treasury bonds. You pay interest monthly or it will continue to accrue on the outstanding balance. However, if the value of your securities drops, your margin will be called. If you do not pay it on time, your securities may be sold generally at a very low price.

Self-financing is an excellent choice for those entrepreneurs who are very confident of the success of their enterprise. It is not for the faint of heart. If your business fails, you may lose your house and car if you used them as collateral. You will have to learn to walk again, and you may well put your family into a financial and emotional hole. However, for entrepreneurs like Mary Kay Ash or me, this is the best investment we could have ever made.

Other people's money (OPM)
Many otherwise capable individuals simply do not have enough capital to finance a business by themselves. If this is your position, do not despair. There are ways to obtain the needed capital.

Banks
Banks are in business to make money, just as you are. Their profit is generated by the interest they charge for lending money. However, most banks consider small businesses, especially start-ups, risky and troublesome. They would prefer to lend money in large amounts to big businesses that are more profitable rather than to hundreds of start-ups and small businesses whose profits, if any, may be minuscule by comparison. This is not the image their advertising promotes, but this is the reality. The only opportunity you have to borrow money from banks is if you have enough collateral to prove that you really do not need the money. Otherwise, you will find a great reluctance on the part of banks to extend you a loan or reasonable line of credit. Given the handicaps a small businessperson has in dealing with a bank, it is obvious that if you want access to the vault, it will require something other than presenting yourself to the banker with a briefcase full of financial and pro

forma statements, business and marketing plans, and a duly completed loan application. The way to get past the wall of noes is to work on the banker, not the bank.

To understand the banker's situation, first you have to realize that all bankers below the level of president and chairman are highly underpaid. They get a paycheck that would send ditch diggers out on strike. This guarantees the bank the right type of sheep that willingly follow the path of least resistance and are frankly too lazy to work hard and too nervous to steal. These junior executives simply want to hang in there long enough to get a bigger desk, more prestigious title, and the right to mingle socially with the community power structure. By nature, most bankers like security, pensions, fancy offices, and titles. Do they have courage or guts? Can they make decisions? Not really. What they prize first and foremost is that which I call *mistake avoidance.* They keep many *outs* and require securities to cover their mistakes, such as personal endorsements by the owner, assignment of life insurance, loans on the business equipment, accounts payable, etc. Under the law, banks come ahead of other creditors. The poor vendor who has provided goods to an unfortunate firm must get in line. The banks come first. It is said that a banker will loan you an umbrella when the sun is shining but wants it back the minute it begins to rain. Here are some ways you can work on the banker rather than the bank:

- Get to know your local public officials like city and county council members, mayor, and state representatives or state senator. Contribute a few dollars to their election campaign. Take them out to lunch and introduce them to your friends and relatives who will pledge their future support. Ask them if they can introduce you to a local banker who specializes in or is at least interested in nurturing small-business accounts.

- Ask your accountant or your lawyer to introduce you to a banker as an up-and-coming entrepreneur with a lot of potential.
- Get to know a member of a bank's board of directors and ask the board member to introduce you to a banker.

With the referral in hand, set up an appointment with the banker. Take your accountant with you, if you can. Having your accountant with you and your positive and bright proposal, you will have a good chance of approval for your loan application. Let the banker know that you are planning to make a lot of money and are looking for a bank to open an account with. But let the banker know he has to compete for your business. Your job is to put the banker on the defensive and arouse his greed to make money working with you. Remember, the way the banker makes money is by making loans. He or she is selling money like you are selling your products and services. But make the banker feel it is in his best interest to do business with you. The only thing you can do for the banker is to give him or her opportunity to earn your business. If you go to the banker with a good reference and your accountant, the banker will not only try to please you but also try to please the person who referred you to him and your accountant as well.

In banking terminology, there are the six Cs of credit: capital, collateral, capability, character, coverage, and circumstances. Your banker will want to know how much capital your business has to start with and what percentage of it is your own personal investment. What assets do you possess that can be used as collateral for the loan? Based on your experience and reputation, a determination will be made regarding your capability and character. The type and amount of insurance coverage you plan to obtain is another important factor. The general circumstances of your business related to consumer demand, competition, and general economic environment would also be taken into consideration. Your ability to sell your banker on your strengths in the areas of the six Cs will directly affect the outcome of your loan application. Be prepared to demonstrate to the banker that you are a solid citizen. Sometimes bankers, especially in small communities, will bend a little for someone who is active in civic affairs and goes to church on Sunday.

Credit unions

Credit unions generally offer lower interest rates than banks. You have to be a member of a given credit union to qualify for a loan. Credit unions are generally formed around an employer, professional or service organizations, a church group or a fraternal group.

Credit unions generally make short-term loans to their members for such purchases as automobiles, furniture, boats, and office equipment. Most credit unions will lend up to $5,000 for the purpose of buying a computer. If your credit rating is good, a credit union can loan you up to $10,000 on your personal signature.

Your suppliers

Some suppliers can be persuaded to provide you certain items on credit, such as starting inventory or office furniture and fixtures, on a thirty-, sixty-, or ninety-day basis and, in some cases, a longer period. Just ask for it.

Finance companies

Finance companies make loans that the banks and credit unions do not want to take a risk on. They make both secured and unsecured loans for virtually any purpose. But both their processing costs and interest rates are very high.

Venture capital companies (VCCs)

VCCs are privately owned investment companies. They provide funding to new and growing companies for an ownership stake in them. Their long-term goal is to take the company public and recoup three to ten times their initial investment by selling their stocks in initial public offerings (IPOs). You will need a well-organized and winning business plan, or your business needs to be in high-growth mode to attract VCCs' attention.

Small Business Administration (SBA)

The SBA is known as *the lender of last resort*. The SBA, generally, is in partnership with lending institutions like commercial banks. It can guarantee direct or indirect loans made to businesses by commercial institutions. Both types of loans have lower interest rates and longer maturities than those associated with conventional loans. There are costs associated with the transaction. Contact the local SBA district office in your area for details. Be prepared for a lot of paperwork, but in the end, it will be worth it.

Small Business Investment Companies (SBIC)

Small business investment companies are privately owned and operated companies that are licensed and in some cases are financed by the Small Business Administration (SBA). Even though they are independent of SBA, they conform to SBA regulations and are subject to SBA control. Check with your SBA district field office for a list of SBICs in your area.

Factoring

Factoring organizations are those that buy all highly rated accounts receivables at a discount. In some cases factoring companies buy solid purchase orders, invoices, contracts, and even secured loans and notes for immediate cash. Factoring companies have greater experience in credits and collections and generally have larger financial resources than average businesses. Factoring is good only when your business is growing and going well, as it helps you in getting immediate cash, even though you sacrifice a part of your profit. There are pros and cons to factoring. Many financial experts believe you should not attempt factoring unless you cannot acquire the capital you need from other sources. Since factoring organizations take anywhere from 10 to 30 percent of the invoiced amount, your profit is greatly reduced. However, in a fast-growing and profitable business, factoring can be a very useful tool for raising money and keeping cash flowing in your operation.

Leasing

Leasing rather than purchasing can be a sound option for many businesses. For example, you can lease a good copying machine, suitable office furnishings, or new plant equipment and vehicles for a few hundred dollars per month rather than putting up several thousand dollars to buy them. I have been leasing a brand-new forklift worth over $16,000 for less than $400 per month. Every three years, I get a new forklift for about the same amount. Once, I wanted to purchase my used forklift and finance it. However, the monthly payment was more than my rental payment. Leasing has been around for a long time. The lease payments are a regular business expense. If you purchase any machine or equipment, it has to be depreciated over a certain period.

Selecting the right method of financing for your business is an extremely important decision. Picking the wrong type of financing sometimes creates additional obstacles to the success of your enterprise. Take your time, compare all options available, and choose the one that is right for you at the time.

CHAPTER IV

How to Market and Sell Your Products and Services While Acquiring and Retaining Customers for Life

Marketing creates an environment that is conducive to selling your products and services to your customers. To create such an environment, you have to have a consistent theme for your customers to recognize you, your company, and your products and services. The following steps must be taken to achieve that goal:

1. Your company logo distinguishes you from your competitors and therefore must be unique and distinctive.
2. Have a tagline under your logo that explains in a few words what your company does.
3. Letterhead, envelopes, business cards, and invoices should have your distinct logo with matching color coordination on a heavier paper.

4. Create a capability flyer or line card that summarizes what you sell and why the customers should buy from you.

5. In the age of the Internet, it is most important that you have a modern-day Web site.

6. Catalogue your products and services with a separate price list. This helps you and your salespeople if and when you have them.

7. Pens, scratch pads, letter openers, paper-clip holders, and calendars, to name a few are great advertising novelties. Use them.

8. Develop and use a sales manual explaining to your salespeople who your target customers are and how you sell your products to them.

9. Have all your suppliers lined up and prices negotiated in advance. Will you manufacture and assemble at your facilities or sell the products already manufactured and assembled?

10. Pricing your products is an art as well as a science. If you cannot mark up the products at least three times your cost, then you should not sell them. Preferably you should mark up your products by four times your cost. If you purchased a product for a dollar, mark it up to four dollars. The best way to get this type of markup is to private-label the products with your logo and address. By doing this, you not only make a bigger profit, but also build your brand name. If the customers like your product, they will continue buying that product from you. Even though the markup of four times your cost sounds high, for large companies this markup is not good enough. They have to have even larger markups. Most people who have not been in business do not

realize how much it costs to stay in business and make a profit.

11. Find your niche market, and target customers in that market segment. As a start-up, you have to concentrate on a small group or an interrelated customer base. Do not try to be everything to everyone. If you do that, you will be nothing to anybody. Keep your market area small, and work to be number one, two, or three in your area.

12. Join local business and service groups, such as the hamber of commerce, Lions Club, or Optimist Club. When you go to their meetings, act like a host not like a guest. Introduce yourself, be friendly and outgoing, and ask how you can help the members and the organization. Be genuinely interested in the members and the club. Volunteer your time and participate in their activities as much as you can, without taking too much time away from your new business.

After completing the twelve steps outlined above, you are now ready to hit the road and sell your products and services. Given my experience at Chemco, I am more knowledgeable about selling products than services. So I will tell you how to sell your products; if you are selling services, adopt some or all of my techniques and apply them as needed to selling your company's services.

Over the years at Chemco, I have sold cleaning, sanitizing, degreasing, and lubricating chemical products. My target customers have been the following institutions:

1. Nonprofit and spending taxpayers' money (tax money), such as the various departments and facilities of municipalities, counties, and state governments.

2. Nonprofit but spending somebody else's money, such as public and private schools, colleges, and universities,

golf courses, recreation centers, country clubs, VFW halls, American Legion halls, Elks Clubs, Knights of Columbus, and religious institutions.

3. Profit centers but with company buyers spending somebody else's money, namely chain hotels, apartment complexes, condo associations, nursing homes, and hospitals.

How do you find the names of these buyers? You go to the city clerk's office at your local city hall, the county clerk's office in the county courthouse, and the school superintendent's offices for the target customers, and ask for and get a list of buyers for the different departments of that particular institution. These lists are public information and are available to you free of charge. My sales manager, Steve Lake, came up with the following method to find qualified leads:

Step 1: Go to your city or county library Web site. In my case, it is the St. Louis County Library Web site (www.slcl. org).

Step 2: At the home page at the top and slightly to the right, you will see a list of options, beginning with Home and About SLCL. Locate and click on Databases.

Step 3: You will see "Quick Catalogue Search" in your upper right-hand corner. Go straight down to Databases A-Z and click on it.

Step 4: Scroll down a short distance and you will see the letters of the alphabet in blue, click on the R.

Step 5: Click on "references.com – Home Access."

Step 6: The next page will be the "Web Access Management Login" page. Type in your last name and library card number in the appropriate spaces and hit Submit. This will get you into the database.

Troubleshooting – Every now and then you may get a Google message saying that the link is broken. If this happens, click the back key on your toolbar and then click your forward key on the toolbar. Repeat until you get a connection. You usually don't have to do this more than six times.

Now you are ready to make a sales call. Here are a few things to keep in mind when you are making sales calls. If you neglect any one of them, you will waste a lot of time talking to the wrong people about the wrong products. So far, nobody has been able to figure out any way to replace wasted time. So use your time effectively. Here is how:

- *Organize your next day every night.* With the help of your list of potential customers that you obtained, using the Yellow Pages and city street maps, make a list of sixteen calls for the next day. Organize the calls in a geographical sequence to save time so you can see at least six potential customers. During the planning period, think about your friends, acquaintances, and past customers who can see and use your products.

- Before making a call, be sure you have your samples and demonstrating materials ready to show. Also, be sure to have advertising novelties with you.

- *Qualify your customers.* Be blunt and specific at this point. Frittering away your time with unqualified buyers literally takes dollars out of your pocket. Say, "Mr. Williams, you do the buying of maintenance products (or whatever product you are selling) for your department, don't you?" If you get a vague answer, keep asking questions until you have it pinned down. If this isn't the right person, go to the right person. You have to talk to the person who can say yes or no to your proposal that day or within a few days.

- Look for a *MAN* in this case; the MAN can be a woman. MAN means a person with money (M), the authority (A) to spend it, and the need (N) for your products or services.

The theory of a successful sale

Before the invention of the automatic transmission for automobiles, cars came with three manual forward gears, neutral, and reverse. In order to reach your destination, you had to start your car in neutral and then, as you drove, shift from first gear to second gear, and then to third gear. Including neutral and reverse, five gears should be used to close a sale:

- *Neutral gear:* Planning the approach
- *First gear:* Introduction and warm-up
- *Second gear:* Presentation and demonstration of your product
- *Third gear:* Closing the sale by asking for the order
- *Reverse gear.* If you do not get the order on the first close, reverse your presentation to second gear and re-emphasize the features and benefits of your products or services. Then try another shift to third gear and ask for the order.

This selling technique is called *gears of selling* and is widely used in selling specialty chemical and maintenance products. I do not know who first invented this technique. The Levy brothers, owners of National Chemsearch of Irving, Texas, are credited for disseminating this selling technique.

Controlling the interview

You must always control the interview. People buy most in the environment in which they are used to doing business. If a buyer greets you in his or her outer office, suggest moving to a more private office to talk. (Buyers sign orders in their office—not in the hallway). Try to have your prospect see you while both he and you are in a *seated position* in his office. Often, the best method is to pick up your sample case and start walking to the prospect's desk, saying, "I have something here you will want to see." The prospect's normal instinct will be to follow you.

Hint: Before shaking hands with a customer, first put your case on the floor. Then give him a firm two-handed shake. Always keep your sample case loaded with "ammunition": your catalogue, order book, and advertising novelties such as pencils, pens, lighters, pads, key rings, calendars, coffee mugs, golf tees, golf balls, coasters, screwdrivers, knives, and letter openers.

I repeat! Always keep in mind that you have one reason and one reason only to be in your customer's presence—to sell your product and properly service that customer. This reason exists in every call.

Most people don't like to see salespeople. A lot of salespeople have emotional hang-ups about this because they don't really understand the reason why. The reason people don't like to see salespeople in general, and unfamiliar salespeople in particular, is that it is a salesperson's job to *press people to make decisions.* We all tend to put off decisions. After all, when you are pressed to make a decision, you may make the wrong one and get hurt.

Psychologists tell us that most buyers are desperately afraid they will make a wrong decision. When faced with a decision-making situation, buyers become tense and irrational, though they may appear to be calm and confident on the surface.

So while you, like most salespeople, probably have a few butterflies in your stomach before making that first call in the morning, the buyer is a lot more afraid than you are. That is why he or she must build defenses against seeing you. ("Buyer out" can mean "buyer hiding." "Too busy" can mean "too scared.")

Your first job in approaching a buyer is to penetrate these defenses and disarm the buyer. In doing so, you have *one vital advantage.* You *knew* you were going to see the buyer and planned what you were going to say and do. The buyer is unprepared and can only use his few standard, flimsy brush-off techniques, which won't work on you because you are prepared for them.

It is often said that most people are still children. Their bodies just get bigger. Whether that is true or not, I would like you to think of a buyer in a sales situation as a frightened child. What is the first thing you do to calm a child? *You take control of the situation in a warm, confident way* and get the child to sit down where you can talk without distraction. You don't go into some lengthy explanation as to why the child should sit down. You *command* the situation by your manner and actions, take the child by the hand, and *lead him.* Instinctively, the child will follow.

Sound far-fetched? Like it won't work on an adult buyer? The fact is that it is the only thing that *will* work!

Your first job is to *lead* the buyer to sit down with you without a lengthy explanation as to *why.*

So if, as often happens, you make your approach to a buyer in a hallway, in a kitchen, or shop, your first job is getting the buyer to a location where he or she is accustomed to sitting down and talking to people. Here's how: walk up to the buyer, smile, and look the buyer in the eye. Put your bag down. Extend a firm two-handed handshake. Say, "Hello, Mr. Johnson." (You'll have made sure of his name by simply asking someone and writing it down.) "I'm John Williams from St. Louis. How are you today?" Now you suggest going to the buyer's office or desk and then lead the way. There are many ways of doing this with words and actions, which you will have to develop through your own personality. Often the best method is just to pick up your sample case and start walking, saying, "I have something here you'll want to see." The buyer's normal instinct will be to follow you. If you are headed the wrong way, in most cases, the buyer will tell you or he may try to qualify you as to exactly what you are selling, so he will know how to phrase his brush-off. Don't let him!

Buyer: I'm too busy. (Forgive him if he is rude. Remember he is scared to death.)

Answer: (Big smile) You know, Mr. Johnson, I call on men in your position every day. Nobody knows better than I do how busy you are. In fact, that is why I came down here this morning—to show you a way to save time—and money, that I am sure you will want to see. (Start walking toward his office, boiler room, shop kitchen, or wherever you can talk to him in a seated position on a one-to-one basis without distraction.)

Buyer: What are you selling?

Answer:(Big Smile) A method of maintenance that can save you a lot of headaches and hundreds of dollars. It would take me an hour to explain how it works standing here, but I can show you in a few minutes in your office (start walking)

Buyer: What are you selling?

Answer: Oh, a little bit of everything (shaking head with a wry smile), and boy, is the boss on my back. That's why I need to see you this morning. (The humorous answer works as the buyer chuckles with you, walking toward his office)

Use this approach, and you won't sell anything:

Buyer: What are you selling?
Answer: A heavy-duty cleaner and degreaser.

If you are able to approach buyers in their offices, you have already got them where you want them and your approach is simplified. You assume their permission to be seated by slowly lowering yourself into a chair and, at the same time, asking them the first complimentary leading question, going naturally into your warm-up technique. Find something to compliment them about. However, the compliment has to be sincere.

The fly in the ointment in approaching buyers in their offices, sometimes, is that receptionists or secretaries who feel that it is their divine duty to protect the buyers from sales-people often protect them. So you must win their cooperation in order to get in to see the buyers without being qualified as to why you are there, thus inviting a brush-off. In such cases, you must make a friend of these front-desk people. The best method is to present them with a small novelty accompanied with a story that establishes you as a nice guy. If you get them on your side, they will convey to their boss by their choice of words or tone of voice when announcing your presence that they should see you. In nine out of ten cases, if the receptionist has been won over, you will be allowed to see the buyer. There is a world of difference between "Can you see Mr. Williams for a few minutes? He made a special trip from St. Louis to see you" and "There's a salesperson out here. Do you want to see him?"

There remains a nagging doubt in the minds of some sales-people as to their right to push their way into a reluctant buyer's presence. They have not only the right but also the duty to do this. After all, buyers' reluctance to see a salesperson springs from their fear of making a decision. Yet it is these buyers' duty to make decisions. That is their job. Buyers are doing a disservice to their employer if they avoid consideration of products that save their employer time and money; therefore, you are justified in using techniques that neutralize buyers' fears and lead them to an open-minded consideration. Fear has always been the greatest enemy of progress. Civilization would never have progressed if a few valiant men in history had not led people to make a decision about new ideas rather than allowing them to cling to old superstitions and ways. By the same token, America would not have one of the highest standards of living in the world today if it had not been for salespeople who led Americans to make decisions to try new and better products over the years.

First gear

The introduction and warm-up

Remember our first step in calming a frightened child? It was to get the child to sit down. The next step is to distract the child, to draw his attention away from his fears by getting him to talk about things that are interesting and pleasant. Once you have established what the child is interested in, you can tell the child a story that will appeal to his interest. Then give the child a cookie and a glass of milk. The child will have forgotten his fear and think you are wonderful.

From this analogy, we know that the next step after getting the buyer to sit down is to sincerely compliment him (showing your interest) and to lead him to talk about things that are interesting and pleasant. Unless the buyer is warmed up, he will not be receptive.

It is often said that the best salespeople are the best listeners. That is certainly true, though a good salesperson will control a conversation through leading questions and close attention to what the buyer is saying in order to discover every-thing possible about the buyer's interests, needs, and fears. Now armed with this information, the salesperson can use proper and proven techniques to first relax the buyer and then structure the demonstration to appeal to the buyer and finally use *this* knowledge to close the sale.

During the warm-up period, *silence is the salesperson's enemy.* He must always have a leading question on the tip of his tongue to keep the buyer talking. When the buyer discusses his vacation, family, or hobbies, let him talk, and listen to him with a look of respect, sincerity, and excitement.

Here is one typical successful warm-up technique:

Mr. Johnson, you certainly have a beautiful building here. When was it built? (Buyer responds.)

You certainly must be proud of it. How long have you been working here? (Buyer responds.)

I can see by the papers on your desk that they really keep you busy. Few people realize how many problems are involved in running an operation of this size. How many people are employed here? (Buyer responds.)

I can see they really keep you jumping. What do you do when you get a little time to relax? (Buyer responds that he likes to go fishing.)

Where do you usually fish? Have you had much luck this year? (Now that you have found out that he likes to fish, lead him to talk about fishing, which is pleasant and divert-ing for him.)

When you get the leading-question technique down pat, you should be able to get the typical buyer pleasantly relaxed in less than fifteen minutes. The buyer now feels good. He is beginning to like you. You are now going to bring his good feeling to a climax by presenting him with an inexpensive but interesting novelty around which you will weave a story, which will amuse and interest the buyer.

"Mr. Johnson, my boss was in Japan last month and visited a tribe of Samurai warriors. He swears this is their ceremonial sword since it was a midget tribe! No kidding, Mr. Johnson, this does make an excellent letter opener. Please use it with my compliments."

Always try to make the buyer feel important with compliments, sincere praise, and your actions.

Here is another effective approach:

"Mr. Johnson, I want you to have my personal calling card so you will remember me. A person in your position will find this three-color pen most useful. I use the green color for my homework, black for my office work, and red to balance my checkbook at the end of the month. I also have a special pencil for you. As long as you use this pencil, I guarantee, you never make a mistake. Look at it!" (Present the pencil, which has an eraser at both ends.)

What have you accomplished with these approaches? You have complimented the buyer. You have demonstrated your interest in him as a human being. You have had him talk about something interesting and pleasant to him. You have relaxed him. You have amused him. You have made him feel good. His fear of you has vanished. He feels that you are a nice person who is sincerely interested in him. The very least he can now do is be interested and courteous to you as you make your transition into your product presentation and demonstration.

Do not misunderstand this warm-up technique. It does not consist of aimless small talk. It is purposeful and should lead directly to a presentation of your products under favorable circumstances.

To emphasize, assume you have accomplished the first phase of your introduction. It is then important to find a mutual field of interest *between you and your prospect*. Learn to be sincere about your prospect's family, hobbies, and business problems. To find his primary interests, ask leading questions such as the following:

1. How long have you been working here?
2. How did you get started in this business?
3. What do you do in your time off?
4. Have you taken a vacation this year?
5. Ask a question about some particular business problem that you feel your prospect would like to talk about.
6. Phrase your questions in such a way as to require more than just a yes or no answer. Wherever possible, let your customer talk for a few minutes. Remember, the most successful salespeople are the "best askers of questions" and the "best listeners."
7. While the buyer is talking, give him the green or go signals by using phrases like "that's interesting," "that's fascinating," "no kidding," "how about that," "that sounds good," "what do you mean by that," "tell me more about it," "what is your opinion about it," "that's great," "that's wonderful," "that must be fun," or "please repeat that." The proper use of these phrases indicates that you are sincerely interested in the buyer and what he is talking about. In the warm-up stage, the less you talk and the more they talk, the better it is. Make it a fun and pleasant time for both you and the buyer.

This warm-up technique is primarily based on the ideas described in the book *How to Win Friends and Influence People* by Dale Carnegie.

Let the buyer talk about his hobby, vacation, and family from five to twenty minutes, and then go into the transition and demonstration of products. You judge when to begin this stage by the tone of the buyer's voice (he is enjoying—feeling good), gestures, or actions. You should have a feeling for this point so that you can go into your transition and business part of the interview at the appropriate moment. The rule of thumb is that your prospect is warmed up when you are warmed up. When you feel relaxed, your prospect is relaxed.

The idea behind the warm-up is to win over your customer to your side so that he likes you as a person. People don't separate the dance from the dancer nor do they separate the product from the salesperson. Before they buy your product or service they must like you and trust you as a person. If that does not happen, it is very difficult to make a sale to him. The following story explains what I mean:

John and Bill are talking, and John asks, "If a lion suddenly appeared in this room, what would you do?" "Run," Bill replies. "If the lion ran after you, what would you do?" John asks. "I would get on the roof." "If the lion climbed on the roof, what would you do?" Bill has enough with this line of questioning and says, "John stop. Time out. You've been asking a lot of questions. Now let me ask you a question. Which side are you on? Are you on my side or the lion's side?" Your customer does not care how much you know. He wants to know how much you care about his feelings, his family, his vacation trips, and his hobbies. If the customer is not on your side, he will raise so many objections that you will not be able to answer them all. So try to make him your friend before moving to the transition step.

Your prospect will not buy from you for three reasons: no trust, no need, and no money. Out of these three reasons, lack of trust is number one. I give you an example. Say, I give you a stack of genuine $20 bills and ask you to go to a four-way crossing. Every time a car stops, you approach the driver; show him/her the genuine $20 bills and say, "I will give you this $20 bill for only $10. Please give me $10, and I will give $20." Most of the drivers will pass on that offer and drive away. You know, why? Because they don't trust you. Just think about it if you can't sell a $20 bill for $10 without building trust, how can you sell your product or service without it?

The shifting action is sometimes called the *transition* because you are shifting into your actual selling effort. You must develop certain phrases, words, and sentences that will smoothly develop your shift.

For example:

1. "Mr. Prospect, we have a couple of products here that I think you will be interested in."
2. "Mr. Prospect, we call on a thousand churches just like yours. We are well aware that perhaps the greatest single problem you folks have is —"
3. "Mr. Prospect, my company is the fastest-growing company in the industrial and maintenance chemical field. We have been able to grow, and we are constantly striving to make better, safer, more economical, and more useful products for you. One of these products is called—"

Second gear
Presentation and demonstration of your products
(Which will create the need for your products)

You have to give a person a reason to buy your product. No one buys because you just happen to be in the mood to make some money. You must convince your prospect he needs your product because it fills a particular need the prospect has. You must convince your prospect that he has a problem and that your product is the best solution for that problem. For example, a person with $1 million worth of life insurance can be sold more insurance if he is convinced he needs it to protect his estate. A Buick owner can be sold a Cadillac if he is convinced he will get more business because he will have more prestige. Conversely, the Cadillac owner can be sold a Buick if he is convinced he is losing business because his customers don't want to buy from a rich person who apparently does not need their business. If you have *a* product to sell, *make up your mind* to convince your prospects why they need *your* product.

Suppose you find the one in a hundred customers who really does not have an actual problem, no urgent problem at all. *In this case, you shift to the preventive program.* Show your prospect that by not cleaning his electric motors periodically with Chemco DYNA-SOL will create a costly problem someday. Call the school, nursing home, and cafeteria maintenance personnel's attention to the fact that he or she can avoid grease trap and drain problems by using BIO-ZYME or ORANGE SOLV regularly once a week.

Where there is no actual problem, you can assist to prevent the creation of a future problem. If you have good products to sell, make up your mind to convince your prospect of the *benefits* he or she will receive from *your* products. How? By demonstration!

Following is an example of a well-thought-out sales presentation:

Kleenzol (Chemco's all-purpose cleaner)

1. "Since you are responsible for the cleaning of your building, you will want to see a product based on a new theory we have developed in floor cleaning. A clean floor is the first step toward a good building appearance

and sanitation, and Kleenzol, our superior cleaner, will do your cleaning job better and faster." This is a transition sentence bridging the gap between the "open" and the "creating the need" phrase.

2. "You will notice I am going to spray a small amount of Kleenzol on your floor. Actually, Kleenzol may be used in your regular mop buckets or sprayed on your floor in a two-gallon sprayer or in a hand-trigger sprayer. Kleenzol, diluted according to the directions, may be used for normal cleaning of floors, woodwork, and windows. In greater concentration, it will also remove old wax from the floor. I'm going to agitate the solution on your floor with my fingers to show you there is nothing that will hurt your floor or my skin."

3. While you and the prospect are talking, Kleenzol is penetrating the pores of the floor and lifting the dirt into the solution. More than that, the dirt is being uniformly suspended in the solution, so it may be entirely removed by picking up the solution with your wet mop. You say to the prospect, "Notice how Kleenzol holds dirt in suspension, while most cleaners allow half the grime to be redeposited on the surface."

4. "Now I am going to remove the solution by wiping it up with this cloth. After the dampness evaporates, I will show you a floor clean enough to eat your eggs on."

5. "With my white pocket handkerchief, I'll wipe the cleaned spot. Look! Absolutely no dirt. Your floor is 'white handkerchief clean.' "

6. "Now watch when I wipe the handkerchief on the part of the floor not cleaned with Kleenzol."

7. "Here, do this yourself so you can prove to yourself how Kleenzol will help you."

8. "Kleenzol not only cleans your floor, but it also removes spots, grease, and grime from your carpets, painted walls, and wood panels. I'll show you how." Spray Kleenzol on a dirty spot on some carpeting. "I will show you that Kleenzol will not hurt my skin by rubbing it on the spot." Place a paper or cloth towel on the agitated spot. Press it down and show the towel to the buyer with the dirty spot off the carpet. Then say "How does it look to you?" After the positive response, add, "I'll show you how it is packaged."

After you have
1. Made a friendly introduction,
2. Qualified and warmed up the customer,
3. Created a need for your products,
4. Demonstrated your product,
You shift into third gear, ask for the order and—close the sale!

Third gear
Closing the sale

Never try to force the customer to say, "Yes, I'll take the product" because no customer will ever say that and attempting to force it won't help you. Make it easy on yourself and let the customer have your materials without forcing him to make a yes or no decision on whether to buy.

Every successful salesperson uses his personalized methods; here are some thoughts to help stimulate your thinking:

The alternative approach. By using this method, you disregard the possibility that your client is not going to buy anything. It is just a question of what size container he is going to buy. Say, "It is packaged in a fifty-five gallon drum and a thirty-five gallon half drum. Which is better for you, drum or half drum?" Or, "It is packaged four dozen to a case and two dozen to a half case. Which is better for you, a case or a half case?"

The assumptive close. With this approach, you assume that, first, the prospect has decided to buy your products as your warm-up, demonstration, and close have been extremely convincing, and, second, that there is only one size you want him to buy, one size that fits him best—the size that is the most economical for your prospect and pays the highest commission to you: the standard fifty-five gallon size. Alternatively, if the size of the containers has been discussed during the demonstration, again, you do not ask, you just assume that the discussed container will be ordered. So just open your order book, start writing, and say, for example, "I am looking forward to hearing from you personally on my next visit as to how satisfied you are with the product. Do you have any preference as to shipping?"

Simply asking for an order. There are many ways of asking, all of which depend very much on the personality of the salesperson. To mention some possibilities, say, "Allow me to add you to our long list of satisfied customers by sending you our standard fifty-five gallon container." Or, "I would appreciate it if you would give yourself and me a chance to enter into a long and profitable relationship. Allow me to send you our standard fifty-five gallon container!"

The impending event method. You can use this method with success if you have recognized the customer's increasing interest. "Sir, this month we have a special on this product that I do feel is terrific. You will receive, with the standard economy-sized fifty-five gallon container, this two-gallon pump-up sprayer with a list price of $35, free of charge. I'll mark it down now so that you can take advantage of this special offer."

The minor choice close. You can let your customer decide *between two positive alternatives,* in other words, give him a choice between *something and something.* For example, "Kleenzol is packed in fifty-five gallon full drum and thirty-five-gallon half drum containers. Would you prefer the full drum or the half drum?" Or, "We can have this arrive next week or the first of the next month, which do you prefer?"

Sales presentation

Let's see how the gears work in an actual sales situation. Remember, while in neutral, you have prepared yourself; your samples are in order and you are ready to shift.

First gear—approach and warm-up

In the *approach,* give only your name and the city you are from. Do not tell them what company you are with or what you are selling. Thus, if you know the buyer's name, you would say, "Good morning, Mr. Johnson, my name is John Williams from St. Louis. Your name is sir (or ma'am)?" Remember, in the *approach* you are trying to calm the buyer's natural fears. Be friendly, be warm, and *smile.*

After you have introduced yourself, you must *qualify the buyer* to determine if he does the actual buying. Do not be satisfied with a flimsy "maybe" answer. Not properly qualifying a buyer can lead to nothing but heartache when you are ready to close and you are told, "I'm sorry, but I can't buy." Simply and in a straightforward way, ask "You do the buying of maintenance products for your department, don't you, Mr. Johnson?"

Having qualified the buyer, you should next present your *novelty* with a little story. If you merely put the *barrier breaker* on the table and say, "I've got a little something for you," you will have wasted the novelty and spoiled the entire warm-up *approach*. The novelty should be offered with a personal and always humorous narrative that, along with the novelty, would both amuse and interest the prospect.

Now that you have the buyer in a calm, humorous mood, you begin your *warm-up* by paying a sincere compliment. Don't tell a chef he has a modern, well-planned kitchen if it isn't truly so. Ask leading questions of a nature that will appeal to the buyer's pride or interest. Always keep command of the conversation. Do not allow the buyer to ramble on and on. Remember, two or three leading questions should be sufficient to put the buyer in a receptive and calm mood. Let him talk for a few minutes. If you find he is enjoying it, keep him on that subject, always striving to keep him on the positive side of the topic at hand. Never let him be negative. If you can find somebody or something in common that you and the buyer know and enjoy, talk about it. Remember, your customers do not care how much you know, but they want to know how much you care.

You have now presented your *barrier breaker*, led the buyer through a short warm-up conversation, qualified the buyer, and put him in a receptive mood. Immediately go into your *transition*.

It is during the *transition* that you tell the buyer whom you represent and why you are there. Example "Mr. Johnson, I represent Chemco Industries, and we have developed a product called COMMAND for people just like yourself with problems just like yours. Let me prove to you just what COMMAND will do." (Take the buyer gently by the arm, lead him to the demonstration, and close.)

Second gear—Demonstration of product

You will then begin the most important step of your sales presentation—*the demonstration*. This is the *key* to the sale. It must be 100 percent effective, and it must be dramatic. Don't forget the truism any presentation without demonstration is an idle conversation. So demonstrate, and demonstrate with passion. You are on the stage like a magician. During the demonstration, *relate product benefits to the customer's needs*. If a particular benefit of the product could not possibly help solve the buyer's problem, don't even mention that particular benefit. You can demonstrate the product by actual demonstration, or you can dramatize the presentation by reading the text and showing the product label and explaining the benefits that similar customers have enjoyed. If you choose to offer an actual demonstration of the product, do so in more than one spot or place.

During the demonstration and presentation of your products, you should appeal to the five senses of the prospect—sound, sight, touch, smell, and taste—if you can. The more senses you can appeal to, the stronger your presentation will be. If you are selling color copiers, let the prospect use the machine. If you are selling cars, let the prospect test-drive them. If you are selling computers, let the prospect use and see the benefit of them. You can use photos, videos, and even charts and graphs to show the benefits of intangible products such as insurance and financial products.

Third gear—closing the sale

After an effective demonstration, you will receive a *buying signal*. A buying signal is any expression of interest in the product. It may be a change of expression, a question, or a simple exclamation.

When you receive your first buying signal, immediately start your *close*. We use an assumptive close. In other words, you assume that the customer is going to buy the product, and you begin to write up the order. The only question that has to be answered is how much. This must be done immediately on the first buying signal. If the buyer is not quite ready, he will make an objection. Answer the objection, and you will receive another buying signal. Close again. Remember, in some cases you may have to make four or five closes before the order is *signed,* especially when you are working with a new account.

The final step, which must be followed throughout the presentation, is this: Smile!

Objections and Rebuttals

More than 90 percent of all objections by prospects are really excuses, stalls, or brush-offs. What they are really saying amounts to, "You haven't made me a friend, why should I buy from you?" or "You haven't demonstrated to my satisfaction what this product will do for me personally." Faced with an objection, you must answer it easily and effectively before proceeding to either resell yourself or resell your product, or both, as the situation may require, leading up to another close.

Actually, an objection is an essential part of most closes. It helps you pinpoint the real reason for the customer's reluctance to sign the order you have written. Once you understand what this reason is you can focus on it, and either eliminate it or not. You are not going to close every order, but your percentage will be much better if you understand the real reason why the customer really doesn't want to buy.

Sometimes, the best way to answer an objection is with a question. Remember how the leading-question technique was used in the warm-up to find out what a customer's interest might be? In the same way, you can use leading questions to get to the bottom of an objection that may be vague on the surface.

Once in a while, a buyer will really stump you with an objection that you haven't heard before. In a case like this, you need a little time to think. Here's a phrase that will give you time. "Mr. Johnson, let me ask you this..." and look studious and serious and hold him with your gaze until you can think of something to say. This can give you as much as five seconds, which is all the time a real salesperson needs.

Here are sixteen of the objections most commonly met by salespeople in the cleaning-chemical industry, along with some ideas about how to handle them. You may come up with better answers (or better questions), and if they work for you, use them.

1. The number one problem for new salespeople is the **put-off** *phrases used by prospects, such as "When are you coming back?"* There is one thing I can promise you: if you can't figure out a good answer that will eliminate this stall, you will never see your prospect a second time. The obvious answer puts you right in your prospect's trap. If you say, "I'll be back in six weeks," he will say, "Fine, I'll consider your products then—probably give you an order." This really means that your truthful answer puts you right out in the cold. Six weeks from now, you have to do the same selling job all over. The prospect has forgotten you: he has bought from someone else and will say to you, "I'm going to buy this from you, when are you coming back?" *And probably, you never will sell him!* However, if you learn to answer the stall as follows, you will be a winner: "Sir,

I will be back and wish I could say just when, but my territory is so extensive that I simply don't know. But since you will run out of my product before I return, I don't want to be penalized by not being here on the right day—so with your permission, I'll just put the product down for shipment so that it will be on hand when you run out and you won't run the risk of being empty-handed."

Reread that paragraph—*it is extremely important.* Another answer to "When are you coming back?" is "Everyone asks me that, and unless I get a chance to let you see how good my product is now, I might never have the chance to come back." This could be a "kidding" type of answer but should be followed with another strong close.

Still another answer: "Mr. Johnson, I have quite a large territory, and it may be some time before I pass this way again on my regular schedule. Even then, all I could do would be to show you once more how this product would make your life more pleasant. Why wait?"

Every time you answer an objection, go back to your closing question. "Which is better for you, drum or half drum? Which is better for you, case or half case?"

2. *"Leave me a sample and I'll think about it."*

"I'm afraid that would put me out of business, Mr. Johnson. This is the only sample I have. Let me show you how this works on" (Redemonstrate.)

3. *"That looks like a good product, but we already have plenty on hand."*

"Of course you do, Mr. Johnson. As I already pointed out to you, this product has many advantages over ordinary products, but the true test of its merits is when you use it yourself. Try a small container of it in part of your building. Compare it with the material you are now using, and I am sure you will want to standardize on my product when you buy next time. Which is better for you, case or half case?"

4. "I have been buying the same product for years, and I am satisfied."

"That's not hard to believe, Mr. Johnson. A man like you likes to get problems solved and keep them solved. I'm sure the product that you have been using is a good one and has been doing as good a job as anything on the market. Until quite recently, there just wasn't anything available to do a better job. Now there is." (Redemonstrate and show how effective, fast, and safe the product is.)

5. "I have been buying from the same company for years."

"Fine, Mr. Johnson, a salesperson always likes to hear a prospective customer express loyalty for the companies that do a good job for him. However, this is a product he doesn't have. Let me send a small quantity. Which is better for you, a case or half case?"

6. "I don't use it."

"Mr. Johnson, many of my regular customers for (product name) are people who had never used this product before. You can genuinely improve the appearance of your building by using this product and, at the same time, reduce the cost of your maintenance. Which is better for you to try, case or half case?"

7. "I don't have the money in my budget right now."

"Mr. Johnson, if you were really convinced that this product could save you time and money, couldn't you find a few emergency dollars in your budget?"

8. "We buy only once a year."

Answer 1:

"Fine, Mr. Johnson, when you issue next year's budget to purchase orders for supplies, we'd like to be included. In the meantime, you have a problem that's costing you time and money. I'm going to set up a small introductory order to get you through the interim period. Then, when you place your annual requisition, you'll know exactly how much you're going to need for the coming year. Which is better for you, drum or half drum?"

Answer 2:

"Mr. Johnson, almost all schools buy in the same manner. Here is something that I know you don't have because it's brand-new. What I would like you to do is buy a small amount now so you will see its worth and then you can thoroughly consider it for your yearly purchase. Which is better for you, case or half case?"

Answer 3:

"Mr. Johnson, many institutions buy in the same manner. While I'm here, there may be a few little odds and ends on which you might be running low. Let me take you through my catalogue. There might be something here you may need."

9. "I'm too busy to watch a demonstration."

Answer 1:

"I appreciate that, Mr. Johnson, but the time and money you can save by spending a few minutes with me now will be well worth your while…or I can come back at your convenience. Is this afternoon or tomorrow morning better for you?"

Answer 2:

"That's why I'm here, Mr. Johnson. I know you are interested in a proven way to save time and money!"

10. "Every salesperson that I see claims he had the best product. I've been fooled by too many of you."

Answer 1:

"That may be true, but I'm not an ordinary salesperson. One order is not going to make me rich or poor. What I want is your continued repeat business, and I cannot get that unless you try a small container today."

Answer 2:

"Mr. Johnson, do I look like the sort of person who would try to fool you? (*Your prospect has to say no.*) Of course not, I have a number of products that I'd like to show you in the future, and I wouldn't be able to do that if I made you look foolish on this first order, would I?"

11. *"I've had four salespeople in here already today."*
Answer 1:

"There will probably be five more behind me, but I represent Chemco Industries. We are one of the few basic manufacturers, and our laboratories have developed a product that is so important to you I know you will want to see it."

Answer 2:

"How many of them showed you a proven way to save time and money, Mr. Johnson?"

12. *"We buy from a local source"* or *"We buy from a company that gives us local delivery."*

"This is always a convenient way to buy, Mr. Johnson, but our product is not available locally. None of your local sources can solve this problem, or they certainly would have done so already. Isn't that true?"

13. *"Your price is too high."*
Answer 1:

"Only if it wouldn't do what I'm showing you it will do!"

Answer 2:

"Compared to what, Mr. Johnson?"

14. *"We buy from a local man."*

"That's fine, Mr. Johnson. I'm sure he does a good job for you. But he doesn't have this product."

15. "I can't get my janitor to use new products."

Answer 1:

"Mr. Johnson, you'd be surprised, but that is the same thing I hear in other schools. Let me ask you a question. Does your janitor complain that there is so much work to do that he cannot get to it all? Then, sir, I can help you. With your permission, I would like to demonstrate this product to your janitor. He will quickly see this product can save *him* time and also *you* money. In other words, he can accomplish more work with less effort by using this product. Now, Mr. Johnson, I'm going to show this to your janitor, and if both of you approve, it will be here in a few days for him to start using."

Answer 2:

"That's a real problem, Mr. Johnson, and I can certainly understand your reluctance to fight that battle with an employee who would be hard to replace. If there's one thing I've learned about this business, it's that good custodial help is awfully hard to find. On the other hand, this is a product that might really appeal to your janitor because it will make his work easier and safer. If you don't mind, I'd like to show this product to your janitor and see what he thinks. Maybe I can get him on our side." (This is one of the most welcome objections you can get. If you can pin a buyer on this type of commitment, your sale is virtually assured. Leave the buyer where he is and go find the janitor. Make a quick friend of him and show him how your product will make his life easier. Don't forget to warm him up as you would the man who actually signs the purchase order. In talking with the janitor, you will naturally have an opportunity to see what types of products he uses and to find out what problems may exist that you haven't found on your own. All this information is valuable to you and you should make the most of such an opportunity to learn about your customer and his problem).

16. "We have to take this up with the board (partners, etc.)."

(This is a phony objection. If you have properly qualified your customer, you know and they know that this is a brush-off and you may treat it as such.)

Answer 1:

"Now, Mr. Johnson, that might be true if you were buying a piece of equipment that ran into thousands of dollars. But we're talking about a small investment in a product that can help you do your job better, faster, and safer. Isn't this the kind of decision that your superiors hired you to make?"

Answer 2:

"Mr. Johnson, how long have you been with the city?" (*He will say five, ten, or more years.*) "Mr. Johnson, I know the council follows your recommendations on the use of chemicals, as you are the only one who knows exactly what you need. I am sure you have the authority to order a small quantity of an item such as this. After you see what it does, you can then recommend the purchase of a large quantity."

Since I have sold specialty chemicals, I have encountered every one of these sixteen objections and, as you can see, have devised rebuttals to each one of them. Your product and service may be different, so you may face different objections. Even so, the rebuttals provided here should help you in finding your own answers.

The customer will also frequently give certain basic objections. Many of these are "false objections," which are just the natural reaction of the buyer to resist making a decision. The successful salesperson must have logical answers for these objections. If you remember what an objection indicates on the part of the buyer, by answering these objections you will have automatically returned to a close. This generally is most easily accomplished by making your second close either more assumptive or a minor choice close using smaller quantities than on your original close.

The most successful way to counter the objection is with the "yes, but" method. Whatever the objection, you always agree with it ("yes") and then "but" it. For an example, if the customer says your price of $20 a gallon of Kleenzol is too high, you say, "*Yes*, Mr. Customer, you are right. *But* I forgot to tell you that one gallon of Kleenzol, when diluted with water, makes ten gallons of cleaning solution. That means it costs you only $2 per gallon, which is very low for a high-quality cleaner like Kleenzol. Which is better for you, drum or half drum?"

When you are answering the multiple objections raised by your customer stay calm, cool and collected. Can you visualize a group of swans swimming in a lake or in a beautiful fountain? They look so serene and relaxed on the surface. But if you could see their legs under the water, they are paddling like hell. That's what you have to do—stay focused and close the sale.

Buying signals

As you make your sales presentation, your customer will frequently ask certain questions that indicate his interest. These are buying signals, and you must train yourself to listen for these signals of interest. Professional salesmanship requires intelligence and thought. Many salespeople spend most of their time talking and very little time listening. Train yourself to listen to your customers; they will give you buying signals as you talk and demonstrate your products. As you hear these buying signals, you will know what your customer is really interested in, and this will give you a chance for a much stronger close.

"I suppose," "I wish I could," "It looks good," "If I could," "Maybe I will," and other similar statements will show you that the objection really means "Yes, I'll buy." Buyers often let you know by a comment, a question, a note of interest or enthusiasm in their voice, a gesture, or a facial expression that they are ready to buy. If you read the signals correctly, you will close the sale. Here are some of the buying signals you should listen for:

1. "How much does it cost?"
2. "How is it packaged?"
3. "How is it mixed?"
4. "How long will it last?"
5. "How much would I need?"
6. "Will it deteriorate?"
7. "How much will it cover?"
8. "Sounds good."
9. "Looks good."
10. "Can you use this for such-and-such?"
11. "Looks okay, but I have plenty on hand."
12. "Who in the area uses it?"
13. "When are you coming back?"
14. "Is it safe to use on such-and-such?"
15. "Will it do this or that?"
16. "How much will it cost me?"
17. "How soon can I get it?"
18. "Will it work?"
19. Any other sign of approval from the prospect, such as a nod of approval.

When you hear any one of the buying signals, start writing the order and close the prospect.
Be quick!

Most buying decisions are of a very short duration, so catch them quickly. Always ask, "Which is better for you, case or half case?" Be fast in writing the quantity and name of the product on your order pad. Then ask the buyer, "What is the shipping address?" Once they give the shipping address, they have bought it.

After a product has been sold, write it in your order pad and have it signed by the customer; then try to sell another product. It is important because once your customer has bought one product, he has made a mental commitment to buy from you. So demonstrate and close on another product while he is still in a buying mood. The customer will tell you when to stop. When he does, stop, give him his copy of the order, thank him, and ask for a referral. See that referral at your earliest convenience.

Ten Commandments of Good Selling

1. Know your product. You must know what your product will do before you can sell with confidence and sell your customer on it. Learn to present dramatic demonstrations of your major products. Make it a habit to practice demonstrations in front of family, friends, and associates. Rehearse, rehearse, and rehearse. Remember, *practice makes perfect.*

2. Be prepared. Be sure your written plan to see sixteen people is ready every night for the next day. Before making a call, know what you're going to show and have your demonstrations and selling materials, as well as your advertising novelties, ready to take with you.

3. Warm up and relax. Warm up and relax yourself and your customer. Talk to people in a language *they* can understand and get them to talk about *themselves* and *their* hobbies, family, and vacation, as well as cleaning and maintenance problems, if possible.

4. Qualify. Qualify your buyer—don't waste time with people who can't buy.

5. Glamorize. Glamorize your advertising novelty. Never give a prospect a novelty without telling a funny story.

6. Control. Control the interview and *lead* your customer to be positive and happy.

7. Create the need. Create the need for your product. Get a nod or an agreement on the problem. Then sell the customer on all the product benefits by telling him what he wants to hear, namely, *what's in it for him.* Is the product safe? Will it save time and labor? Will it make the work easier? Then *demonstrate! Demonstrate! Demonstrate!* A presentation without a demonstration is an idle conversation. To help make your point about this product, demonstrate in more than one-way, and more than one place.

8. Listen. Listen for buying signals. Don't ignore them. The moment you hear the buying signal, ask the closing question and begin writing in your order pad.

9. Close. Close in an easy conversational manner. There are many ways to close, such as by leading the customer into it or by using leading questions, which give the customer a chance to justify himself and the purchase. Whatever you do, *close! Close! Close!* In the immortal words of David Mamet's *Glengarry Glen Ross*, "ABC—always be closing." The man who does not *close* at the right time is just an unpaid visitor, not a salesperson. The man who closes makes a lot of money and builds his territory into a high, productive income for his family. Memorize closing questions: "How does it look to you?" I'll show you how it is packaged. It's packaged four-dozen to a case or two dozen to half a case. Which is better for you, a case or a half case? It comes in either a fifty-five-gallon drum or a thirty-five-gallon half drum. Which is better for you, a drum or a half drum?" Once you ask the closing question, do not say anything. Now it's the customer's turn to talk. Be ready and quick about writing in your order pad.

10. Referral. After closing on as many products as you can, warm up the customer again. Then say, "You know what I sell. Do you know anyone else who might want to see and buy these products?" Write the names and phone numbers on the back of your order pad. Call on these referrals as soon as possible. As you see each one, begin again with one to ten of the commandments of good selling until you build a territory that you will be proud of and that will generate a repeat source of income for you and your family.

How to keep your customers for life

It is very difficult, time-consuming, and expensive to acquire a customer. When a customer buys from you, he places his trust in you. In essence, he is buying you along with your products or services. So if you want continued business and referrals from him, you had better treat that customer like your grandmother—with kindness, respect, and prompt service as follows:

1. Send a thank-you card or note. Everyone likes to be thought of as special. The fact that the customer placed an order with you is important to you. Send him a thank-you card or note the same or the next day the order was placed. Once, I had a large quantity of what I called *thank-you grams* and mailed them to each of my customers every night with a personal note about our visit or his hobby, family, or vacation. These notes and cards made a big difference in maintaining a good relationship with my customers.

2. Deliver the purchase promptly. When the customer makes a purchase, his emotions are high about using it. Once you receive the order, expedite the delivery to the customer as soon as humanly possible so that the customer is reassured that he made the right decision by placing his trust in you.

3. Handle complaints properly. When a customer calls with a complaint, it is the best time to lock that customer in with your company for life. He is doing you a favor by calling and complaining. You should worry when your customers don't call because they will tell ten of their friends how bad your company is and start buying from your competition. If the customer is not fully satisfied or is unhappy with the purchase, invoice, or some other matters, you must decide how to remedy the situation in a calm, friendly, and efficient way. Here is the way to handle it:

a. Listen to the customer without any interruption. Let him talk it out.

b. Identify the customer's complaint without being defensive or angry.

c. Thank the customer for calling you and giving you an opportunity to correct the situation.

d. If you do not understand the problem, ask the customer very politely to give you the details.

e. Take the necessary steps to resolve the problem as soon as possible.

f. Do not argue with the customer—even if the customer is upset.

g. Always show that the customer is right in bringing the complaint to you, as you would have done the same thing in his situation.

h. Remember, the customer is always right, even when he is wrong.

4. Build a customer profile card. Successful salespeople value their customers' business and their friendship. They prepare a customer file on each of their customers. Depending on your business, you should have a record of your customers' buying patterns—what they buy, how much they pay, how often they buy, and what they will buy the next time you call on them. In addition, you should have a record of their birthdays, wedding anniversary dates, their family members' names, their hobbies, and their vacation plans.

5. Stay in touch with your customers. Your customers are your bank account. Your customer base is where your income

is coming from. Take good care of them, and they will take good care of you. So stay in touch with them by:
  a. e-mailing and telephoning them periodically.
  b. remembering them on their birthday and treating them to a nice lunch or dinner.
  c. sending them greeting cards on special occasions.

Harvey Mackay in his book *Swim with the Sharks Without Being Eaten Alive* describes how to prepare a sixty-six-question customer profile on each and every customer or client you are doing business with. I believe that the value of the sixty-six-question customer profile is not limited to salespeople. As with all employees, from time to time one or more of your salespeople will retire or leave the company. A customer profile is a way to prevent customers from leaving your company. It gets the successors of the departed employer up and running with a decided timing edge and a much shorter learning curve than would be necessary if the new salesperson had to start from scratch.

The gears of sales processes have been very successful in sales of our products to maintenance and housekeeping professionals in institutional and industrial environments. You may find that you have to modify the Chemco way of selling to fit your company, your personality, and your customers and clients. However, I recommend you stay very close to my way of selling for at least three months to a year for quick success and then modify my way as needed. My approach is very direct and aggressive, and produces fast results. Try it.

As you develop a sales process that is right for you and your business, here are some considerations to keep in mind:
  1. Make a friend before trying to make a sale. Be sincere about your desire to help your customers and try to build a long-term relationship with as many as possible.

2. Enclose your business card with every letter, note, and communication with your customers. Provide a toll-free contact number and your e-mail address.

3. Make sure to motivate your customers to have your company Web site as a favorite (bookmark) on their computer.

4. Thank people in writing for referring prospects to you.

5. Never lie and never bad-mouth your competition.

6. Contribute more than just your products. Provide industry updates, helpful hints, creative ideas, and business advice.

7. Participate in and become a member of industry organizations that your customers belong to.

8. Donate money and/or advertise in your customer's charitable activities and fund-raising efforts.

9. Stay available to your customers for their questions and comments.

10. Get periodic feedback from your customers regarding the quality of your product and service.

CHAPTER V

How to Win Big in Your Business

Build your desire to succeed

Winning big in your business and winning big in your life begins with your thought process, your desire, and your mode of action. The truly rich are those who know the creative power of their inner thoughts and who continue to impress their thoughts of abundance and prosperity to their subconscious mind. Psychologists tell us that our brain is made of two parts—conscious mind and subconscious mind. The conscious mind takes up about one tenth of our brain and subconscious mind takes up the remaining nine-tenths. Any new information and knowledge that we receive is recorded quickly in our conscious mind but forgotten just as quickly. By spaced repetition we can lock the recently received worthwhile information and knowledge in our subconscious mind. Once in our subconscious mind, the information is permanently recorded and never forgotten. Your desire to succeed, your dreams and goals, and your plan of action to achieve them must be inscribed indelibly in your subconscious mind by spaced repetition and daily affirmation.

Believe. You really believe that wealth in the world, especially in the United States of America, is vast and enormous like an ocean. You can get as much of this huge wealth as you desire and are willing to prepare yourself for. You are not competing against anybody but against your own thinking and imagination. You have to think *big* for the big things to happen in your life. Even as you experience success or lack thereof in your business, a lot of things may go wrong. But those mishaps should not deter you from your path and should not sow the seed of doubt within you. People you depended on may not come through the way you expected; do not let that have an adverse effect on your thinking. Do not sink into despair—just become more determined to succeed!

Stay positive and take comfort in your knowledge and confidence. You will find that things will eventually work out. Just as a seed placed in the ground produces hundreds of seeds if nurtured with care, so the person who fully attends to the limitless riches of his mind will possess more of the world's goods. You have just started your business: now you cultivate it. Realize that you can have all the riches you desire without taking anything away from anyone else. Just as there is no shortage of air, there is no shortage of riches in the universe.

Nature is lavish, extravagant, and beautiful. Think clearly about what you want, visualize it vividly in your mind, and then tell yourself you already have achieved it. When you mentally accept something as true, your subconscious finds ways to bring it to you. Your dominant attitude is your real boss. Your thoughts are your masters and determine your attitude. Think constantly about the ideas of harmony, success, and prosperity. Nourish them emotionally. The outside is the reflection of your inside. Keep building your inside daily with good ideas, good

DOC YADAV

thoughts, and good planning. Expect the good things to happen and they will. It's the law of nature. When you sow well, you reap well. Opportunity is always knocking at your door. Form a clear picture of what you want and feel it emotionally, knowing that the power of your subconscious will make it real for you. This is your opportunity to think, dream, plan, and act boldly. If you fail to take action, there is no one to blame but yourself. Take the responsibility of your own actions and of your own success or failure. Cease blaming others—your competitors, the government, taxes, and world conditions. You are an entrepreneur and a business owner. Think big, visualize success, truly feel that you are successful—and the law of attraction will do the rest. You get attracted to and see plenty of what you are sold on and committed to.

At this point, let me ask you a question: what kind of automobile are you driving? Say you are driving a Ford Taurus. Before you bought that Ford Taurus, I'll bet you rarely noticed a Taurus on the road, did you? The moment you bought your Taurus and drove it from the dealer's lot, it appeared to you that everybody and his brother were driving Ford Tauruses. Do you know what happened? You made a commitment, and you followed through on it. The same is true for riches and opportunities in your life. Once you make a commitment, you see the opportunities all around you.

Build your imagination to achieve
Imagination is one of the primal faculties of your mind. It has the power to project and to clothe your ideas, giving them visibility on the screen of space. Imagination is the mighty instrument used by great scientists, artists, inventors, writers, and business tycoons. Scientists and artists, through their imagination, penetrate the depths of reality and are able to reveal the secrets of nature.

When the world says, "It is impossible, and it can't be done," the person with imagination says, "It is done." It is just as easy and far more interesting for you to imagine yourself as rich and successful in your business and in your life than it is to dwell on poverty and failure. If you wish to bring about the realization of your ideas or ideals, form a picture of fulfillment in your mind and constantly imagine the reality of your desire. This way, you will actually force into being what you imagine as true—what already exists in your mind—and if you remain faithful to your ideal, it will one day be real in your life. The master architect of your imagination will project on the screen of visibility that which you impress on your mind. Jim Rohn, a great motivational speaker, explains this phenomenon as follows: imagine your mind as a slide projector, your life as a big (100-inch) screen, and your thoughts as slides. If you put a 2-by-2-inch slide of negative pictures (thoughts) in the slide projector (mind), it will project that small slide of negative images onto a 100-inch screen (life). The opposite is also true: if a slide of positive pictures is placed in the projector (mind), it will project a large picture of positive images on the screen of your life. It is up to you what kind of thoughts you allow to be placed in your mind. It is really true: change your thoughts, and you will change your world.

Your thought pattern has more power than you think. Let me give you an example. Say you are driving on a four-lane highway. You look toward the driver who is driving next to you in the other lane. That driver will invariably look toward you. You are not sounding your horn; just looking toward that driver has drawn his attention. How many times have you been thinking about your mother and she calls you right at that moment? It is very important for your progress that you understand and respect the power of your own thoughts and how much they affect you and the people around you.

Lest you doubt the power of imagination, consider that it is from the imaginative mind of man that: radio, television, steamboats, automobiles, copiers, airplanes, computers, the Internet, the iPhone, lifesaving drugs, and all other modern inventions came about. Your imagination is the treasure house of infinite expansion of your business and your life's riches. You can picture your business to be big, with additional branches and employees. You can make others rich by seeing them, as they want to be seen: radiant, responsible, and successful as your associates and partners in your business. Remain faithful to your mental picture, and it will come to pass.

You are what you imagine yourself to be. Imagine yourself to be rich, happy, and prosperous, and all the riches of the universe will gravitate to you. If you dream it, you can do it. Dreams are built on the wings of hope and expectation. Hope for and expect the best, no matter how grim the outlook. Give yourself time. Time has enormous power to heal your hurt, disappointments, and despairs. Have faith in yourself and your ability to overcome any obstacles. Inner attitude, expectations, and results almost always converge harmonically. How many times do we say, "I knew that would happen," when something bad happens? When something good happens, how often do we say, "I knew that would come true?" We are right both times because what we expect will happen almost always does happen.

As we learn to discipline our minds, our job is to be sure that what we are expecting is what we want to occur. Powerful forces within and outside you are set in motion by your attitude of expectation. Productive attitudes can be cultivated by your continuous awareness and repeated trials. This attitude of expectation, which is accepted by your subconscious mind, will be what produces results in your life. Always keep before you the image of what you want to experience in your business and in your life. See it, feel it, live it, love it, and develop in your mind the mood of already *owning* your cherished dream then act from that starting point.

The smartest person of the world resides within you

There is an old Hindu legend that when the Brahma God, creator of the universe, finished building the human body, he was not sure where to place the god-head—the power of thought, reasoning and wisdom—so that it would not be easily accessible to everyone. Rather than assuming this awesome responsibility himself, the Brahma God called all other gods to a gathering of the greats in a beautiful conclave. The God of Truth, God of Love, God of Peace, God of Spirit, God of Principle, God of Wisdom, God of Energy, God of Courage, God of Action and all other gods arrived. The Brahma God opened the august gathering, welcomed all the gods, and asked for suggestions where to hide man's godhead? One god suggested that the god-head be placed on the highest peak of the mountain, Himalaya. The Brahma God said, "Don't do that. Man will climb the highest peak of the Himalaya, will find the god-head, and misuse it." Another God suggested, "Bury the god-head deep in the ground." The Brahma God said, "Don't do that either because man will dig the ground, find it, and misuse it." Another God suggested, "Sink the god-head to the bottom of the ocean." The Brahma God said, "Don't do that because man will dive, find the god-head, and misuse it." After spirited debate, heated discussion, and many more suggestions, the God of Wisdom stood and suggested, "Hide the god-head in man's head." With a huge grin, the Brahma God said, "That's right. I will hide the god-head in man's head because only a few men will ever think to look for it within themselves." That's where the god-head—the source of inspiration, courage, and wisdom—has been forever. Look within yourself, find your godhead and realize the source of your creative force. The smartest person in the world resides within you.

You are the architect and the builder of your own fate
The process of building your fate starts with your thought process. It is called the cycle of the self-fulfilling prophecy. It works as follows:

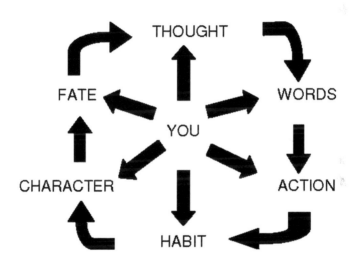

When you think (thought) of doing something, you verbalize (words) internally or externally, and then you act (action) on it. People are creatures of habit, and if things are done long enough or repeatedly, they become habit-forming. You can do things by formed habit without even thinking about it. You know the saying Man is a creature of habit. Your habit forms your character, and your character is what you do when no one is watching you. Once you build your character, people around you know what type of person you are, and they reward or punish you accordingly. They promote you or demote you, trust you or distrust you, honor you or insult you, and that eventually becomes your fate. In this way, you build your own fate by controlling and directing your thoughts and thought pattern. I often tell this story, which I read somewhere, to illustrate the power of your thoughts. John and Martha had a hamburger stand during the Great Depression of the 1930s. They served high-quality, thick-and-juicy hamburgers during the lunch hour; their hamburgers were so good that people were lined up thirty to forty deep every day. Some Sundays, the line was longer than seventy to eighty people. John and Martha had a great business, and they were making very good money. They sent their only son, John Jr., to an Ivy League college, where he read all the newspapers and heard the hourly news broadcasts on the radio. During one holiday, John Jr. came home and asked his parents how their business was doing. John Sr. said, "Son, if our business was any better than this, it would have killed us. Your mom and I are very busy and happy serving our customers. As a matter of fact, son, the line of customers to buy our burgers is growing longer and longer every day." Hearing that, John Jr. was surprised, and said, "Pop, don't you know that we are in the middle of a great depression? A large number of Americans don't have jobs, banks are failing, and some bankers are even committing suicide by jumping out of buildings." John Sr. said, "Your mom and I are so busy making high-quality, thick-and-juicy hamburgers and serving our customers, we don't have time to read newspapers or listen to the radio. Our business is doing great, and we are making good profit every day." John Jr. persisted and showed his parents some pictures of people in unemployment and soup lines, bankers jumping out of buildings, and men offering to work for food. Those pictures started changing the thinking of John and Martha. As a result, they started cutting back on the amount of beef, tomatoes, onions, and other ingredients in their hamburgers. The quality of their high-quality, thick-and-juicy hamburgers started going down, and the line of customers for their hamburgers began to dwindle. One day they didn't have a single customer. John and Martha closed their stand, came home, and told John Jr., "Son, you were right; we are in the middle of a great depression."

Build your goals and your goals will build you

Goals are dreams with deadlines attached to them. Top-level athletes, successful businesspeople, and high achievers in all fields of endeavors use goal-setting techniques. Your goals provide you the long-term vision and short-term motivation. Your goals help you organize your time and resources so that you can achieve the most important things in your life.

The 1957 graduating class of Yale University was interviewed about whether members had specific goals and a written plan of how to obtain their goals. Less than 3 percent had a set of goals with a written plan. Twenty years later the class of 1957 was interviewed about their successes. The study showed that the 3 percent of those students who had written a set of goals were worth more than the combined worth of the 97 percent of the class who did not.

You can divide your lifetime goals into three categories as follows:

1. Long-term goals. More than ten years in the future. Long-term goals provide the overall perspective and the direction of your life and your business. Steven Covey has written, "Start your journey with an end in mind," adding, "If you were dead and your best friend, family members, your preacher, and coworker were giving the eulogy, what would you like them to say about you?" Design and work toward making your life worthy of these eulogies. Write your own epitaph. Long-term goals help you be what you want to be in your life. The same is true for the business or the company you started. Remain true to yourself. Make sure that the goals you set for your life are goals you genuinely believe in and goals you truly want to achieve. These are your lifetime goals—not your parents', friends', or even your business partners'—for you and your business, so they had better be what you want you to have. Be very specific about your goals and make them time bound, meaning your goals should have a date when you want to achieve them.

2. Midterm goals. Three to five years. After your lifelong and long-term (ten-plus years) goals are set, you can decide what you want to achieve personally and for your business within the next three to five years.

3. Short-term goals. Daily, monthly, and yearly personal and business goals.

Writing about goal setting on entrepreneur.com, Ray Silverstein, the renowned small-business expert, set out his SMART technique for setting goals:

S = Specific: Make sure your goals are concrete, concise, and attainable.

M = Measurable: Your goals should be such that they can be measured monthly, quarterly, and annually.

A = Achievable: You should have faith that you can achieve your goals.

R = Realistic: Your goals should be realistic—not just dreams and hot air.

T = Timely: Give yourself a deadline to achieve every one of your goals.

As you decide your long-term, midterm, and short-term goals, write them down on a piece of paper; set out what you want to achieve for your personal-growth goals and your business-growth goals, and assign each goal a date (deadline) as to when you would like to achieve them. Even better, write them down as if you already achieved them. Then read them daily to yourself, feeling the pleasure of achieving them as you visualize them in your mind's eye. They are called *affirmations*. When you repeat and memorize your affirmations every day, your subconscious mind accepts them as true and energizes your actions for achieving them. It is said that winners must have two things: well-defined goals and the burning desire to achieve them.

By knowing precisely what you want to achieve, you know where you have to concentrate your efforts, time, and resources. When you achieve a goal, take the time to celebrate and reward yourself. Failure to meet your goals does not matter as much as long as you learn from it. As time goes on, your short-term, midterm, and long-term goals may change. Adjust them regularly to reflect your progress personally and financially. All this helps you build self-confidence and belief in your vision.

Your business can grow only to the extent that you grow. To have is to be. Before you have wealth, you have to be wealthy mentally. If your wealth comes to you before you are ready to receive it, the wealth will get away from you.

You have heard about lottery winners—people like a truck driver, a waitress, a busboy, a factory worker, and down-to-earth folks who win $1 million, $2 million, and even $100 million in various lotteries. The surveys of those multimillion-dollar lottery winners have found that within seven to ten years, most of them are broke and/or in bankruptcy. You may wonder how they managed to go broke after they had so much money. A lady in my neighborhood had won lotteries not once but twice—over $20 million each time. She lived in a $1 million home with several expensive cars. Within five years, she was behind on her house payments. The bank eventually took over the house. She was without a place to live. What happens to people like her sounds bizarre, but it follows my theory that although they had millions of dollars, they were not ready to be millionaires. They got ahead of themselves. They got money before they were ready to receive it. They lost all that money and went back to driving a truck or being a waitress, a busboy, or a factory worker. But this time, they did not enjoy their work anymore; they were spoiled by their suddenly developed taste of money.

I wonder how megarich sports figures like Mike Tyson can go broke after making over $200 million in his career. He is not alone. You might know a great football player, baseball player, or basketball player who literally made millions in a few years and, within ten years, lost it all. My analysis is that these players are talented and brilliant at their game, but they are hollow inside. Their body has grown, but they are still children inside. They have millions of dollars, but they have not grown to be a millionaire, and they do not have a millionaire's mind. You cannot have something that you are not. Before you *have*, you have to *be*.

When you earn the money by working for it, and as your income is growing, you are also growing with it. You know the value of money as you work hard to earn it. You spend it wisely, and you respect and enjoy the things your money buys for you. For example, if you bought a $100 pair of shoes for yourself and, let us say, you spent two hours to earn that $100, then that pair of shoes is worth two hours of your life. It's no wonder that you will take care of that pair of shoes a lot better than if the same pair of shoes was given to you by someone, free of charge or even as a gift.

A lot of people believe that if they can make more money, they will enjoy their work. But it really is the other way around. If they enjoy their work, they will, in most cases, make more money. The secret is to figure out what you really enjoy doing without the potential of financial rewards. During December 2008, my wife and I were in Disney World with our daughter, son-in-law, and two grandsons—a five- and a two-and-a-half-year-old. I was amazed at the construction, lighting, and unique architecture of the castle in the Magic Kingdom, and I thought of Walt Disney and his passion to build a multimillion-dollar empire around a mouse. His love for the work he did was greater than the money he made in his life. Every time I pass by a McDonald's, I think of Ray Kroc, who built a hamburger stand empire with his passion and love of serving billions of people with low-cost, clean, and quality hamburgers. Walt Disney, Ray Kroc, and people like them make history with their passion for their work. Develop the passion for the work you do.

It is said that successful people work harder on themselves than on their job. Working on yourself means reading about successful people and reading self-help books, attending training classes and seminars, listening to cassettes and CDs in your car while driving around, reading your daily affirmations about how to improve yourself, and thinking about your personal and business goals, and determining your plans to achieve them. This has to be done on a daily basis. This reminds me of a story about two woodchoppers, Tony and John. Tony was in his late fifties and an excellent firewood chopper. John was in his early twenties, very healthy, and ambitious. Tony could chop and pile up more wood on a daily basis than John. No matter how hard John worked, he could not come close to chopping as much wood as Tony did. John was getting frustrated with his performance. He went to Tony and asked him what his secret was. Tony asked, "John, can you tell me what you do when you go home?" John said, "Tony, you know, wood chopping is hard work. After work, I stop at a neighborhood bar, have a couple of beers, go home, have my dinner, watch a little TV, and go to bed. The next day, I am here." Then Tony said, "Let me tell you what I do after work. Even before I enter into my home, I sharpen my axe every day in my garage, and then I do everything you do.

When did you last sharpen your axe, John?" John had no idea when he had sharpened his axe last. You have to sharpen your skills every day to achieve your financial freedom.

In summary, I ask you to write your personal and business goals with deadlines to achieve them on a piece of paper. Then divide them into short-term, midterm, and long-term goals. Read and reread them daily in the beginning and as often as possible thereafter, and compare them with the actual results every quarter and every year. Learn from your successes and failures. Adjust your strategies to meet the challenges ahead. Always remember, no victory is final, and no defeat is terminal.

Planning is the blueprint to achieve your goals

A business plan is the road map for how to achieve your goals and fulfill your dreams of being a successful entrepreneur. Here are the basics of a business plan:

1. Your company. What will your company do and what products and services will it provide? What is the expertise and experience you have in this type of business?

2. Your target market. What are your customer demographics? How big is this market? Who are your competitors? What edge do you have over them? How will you get those customers to buy from you rather than from your competitors?

3. What is the break-even point? That means how much you will need to sell per month to pay all your bills! Any amount over that point generates profit for your company.

4. What is your marketing plan? How will you reach your customers—direct sales force, commissioned representatives, telemarketing, Internet sales, direct mailing, or a combination of these?

5. How much money do you need to get started? What is your sales projection for the first three years, and what would your bottom line (profit) look like?

There are many books, computer programs, and Web sites available for business planning. Among them are Business Plan Pro software and Onepagebusinessplan.com, and there are many more programs to help you. Search on www.google.com using the key words *business planning*, and you will find a lot of books, CDs, and programs that you can use. No matter what you do, have a written business and marketing plan. If you are looking at bank loans or SBA loans, you will have to do it. Even if you do not go for financing, you should have them for your own guidance.

During the planning process, you have to understand the core business cycle, which is universally applicable no matter which type of business you are in or whatever your business model is. The core business cycle is as follows:

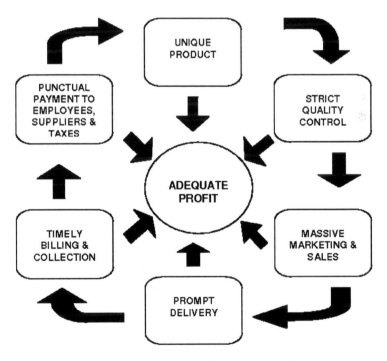

CORE BUSINESS CYCLE

Unique product

Your product has to have unique features that separate it from the products generally available on the shelf. For example, is your product safer, greener, faster, cheaper, better, or more convenient than those sold in big-box stores like Wal-Mart, Costco, Home Depot, and Lowe's? Because of their huge buying power, they can sell the products at a price cheaper than the price you pay just to purchase them from the manufacturer. If that product is already sold at those stores, you do not want to sell it. Search, find, or make your product different.

Strict quality control

Quality control means that your product has the same color, taste (if it is edible), smell, feel, and shape every time. If not, then it has to be discarded. One of the reasons that McDonald's restaurants do not fail is because of the strict quality control of their products. Every time you buy a Big Mac, whether in Jacksonville, Illinois, or Jacksonville, Florida, it tastes the same. When you are hungry for a Big Mac, you almost have its taste in your mind and mouth before you buy and bite into it. In the case of the Big Mac, you will get the same taste every time. It is amazing, considering that local suppliers of buns, beef, and other ingredients are different. Facing all these variables, McDonald's delivers the same Big Mac every time. You have to do be as consistent with the products or services you deliver to your customers; if your quality is consistent, your customers will continue to patronize your business. It does not have to be high class or low class, but the same class every time.

Massive marketing and sales campaign

Even if you have a unique product, and it is produced under strict quality control standards, you still have to market and sell your product, and that effort has to be massive and prolonged on a repeated basis. So you have to have free and paid advertising, mailings, public relations, phone calls, e-mails, and face-to-face presentations on a one-on-one basis or in a public forum. Cut down the time between marketing campaign and obtaining the orders for your products. Read and use the techniques explained in chapter 4.

Prompt delivery

Once you receive the order for your products, ship and deliver the order promptly. When the customers place their orders, they are very excited about your product, and they want to use the product immediately. If you get the product to customer quickly and it delivers the benefits promised to your customers, they can be the best source of advertising for your product. Word of mouth is the best form of advertising.

Timely billing and collection

If you are working with the public, you want to charge buyers for their purchase before you deliver it to them. In this case you have to be ready to accept MasterCard, Visa, and Discover, which are very easy to set up. If you are selling to industries and institutions, you bill them the same day or the next day after the order is shipped. This is very important—you have to have a procedure in place for same-day billing, monthly statements, and phone calls for the over-sixty-days' unpaid invoices. In most cases, 100 percent of the amount of your over-sixty-days' unpaid invoices is 100 percent profit. Within sixty days, you have paid your suppliers, your employees, and your overhead and freight charges for the shipment. You have to be very strict in collecting. Cash flow is the lifeblood of your business.

Punctual payment to your employees, suppliers, and taxing authorities

If you follow the plan outlined in this book, you will not have a cash-flow problem. Pay your employees' market rate or even better wages on the predetermined day or date. That gives them security and a safe feeling to come to work for you. In most cases, your suppliers will give 1 percent or even a 2 percent discount for paying their invoices within ten days. Take that discount, which can be a 12 to 24 percent return on your money. If some suppliers do not give you any discount, pay them after thirty or more days. You do not want to argue with the local, state, and federal agencies for sales taxes; Social Security taxes; federal, state, and local personnel taxes; and corporate taxes. Pay them on time; otherwise, their late charges and fines can be outrageous. It is very difficult to argue and fight with them. Please make sure to sign all the payment checks yourself. All the checks should have the corresponding invoices. In the case of products, you should have a signed packing slip, which means that the products ordered have been received. Check them before signing the check for payment.

Adequate profit

Have good accounting systems like QuickBooks, Peachtree, and others installed on your computer. All the business transactions of your business should be handled through these accounting programs. By doing so, you can get your profit-and-loss statement within a matter of minutes. Run your profit-and-loss statement weekly, monthly, and quarterly, and compare it against the same period of the previous year. See that you are making a profit: if not, make necessary changes and improvements in your operations so that you are making a profit quarterly and annually. The key is that you are making a profit, and the larger is the profit, the better-managed operation you have. Profit makes it possible for your business and you to grow.

There is a funny story related to profit. Ron and John were talking with each other about how they could become rich. Ron said, "Well, we have no college degrees, and we are not lawyers, doctors, or accountants who make big money. How can we get rich?" John replied, "Businesspeople make big money. We should go into our own business and get rich." They agreed on a business idea to buy watermelons in Biloxi, Mississippi, and sell them at the Soulard Farmer's Market in St. Louis, Missouri. They rented a Ryder truck to drive to Biloxi, and bought a truckload of watermelons for $1 each. They drove all night and were back at St. Louis early the next morning. They put up a stall and started selling watermelons at $1 each. At that price, all the melons were sold out by 2:00 P.M. Ron and John were elated by the fast sale of their product. Then they figured out their income and expenses. Ron said, "John, we are in a darn good business, but we did not make any money. As a matter of fact, we lost money." To that, John said, "Do not worry, Ron. Next time we will rent a bigger truck and make money on volume."

You have to charge enough for your product so that you can earn a decent profit; otherwise, you will go out of business very soon.

A lot of small businesspeople are too timid and sell their products or services at a very low price. They are afraid that they will lose the customers if they charge market or above-market prices. I'd like you to consider this: if you drive past a fast food restaurant and see a Help Wanted sign in the window, would you be satisfied with a job there? I am sure your answer is no. Why not? Because they do not pay enough. Is that right? Well, then why would you sell your products or services to customers who do not let you make a decent profit?

Leave them alone, and sell to somebody who appreciates your business and is willing to pay you a reasonable price so that you can make a profit.

Profit is a must. There can be no security for any employee in any business that doesn't make money. There can be no growth for that business. There can be no opportunity for the individual to achieve his or her personal ambitions unless the company makes money.

Unless you have a large sales volume, which is difficult to attain in the beginning, you have to learn how to add value to your products or services so that you make a good profit on a small sales volume. Think about parochial or private schools. They are competing against the public schools. With public schools, there is no tuition, buses are free, textbooks are free, and, in some cases, even lunches are free or at a subsidized low price. Compare that with parochial and private schools. Parents have to pay a hefty fee, take their children to school, pay for textbooks and lunches, and then bring their children home every day, five days a week. Against this type of competition from public schools that are free, parochial and private schools should fail. But they are not failing—they are prospering. Any child can go to a public school, but there is stiff competition and children go through a lot of hoops to be admitted to parochial and private schools. Figure out how these schools do it and use the same principles in your business.

Have you ever bought bottled water? For a pint of bottled water, in some cases I have paid over $1.50. That means a gallon (eight pints) of bottled water cost me almost $12. We complain long and loud about $4 per gallon of gasoline, but we gladly pay $12 per gallon for bottled water. I jokingly say that the United States is the only country where water costs more than gasoline. How about Starbucks coffee for more than $4 versus $1 at McDonald's? Our auto giants—General Motors,

Ford, and Chrysler—are hurting (GM went bankrupt) and looking for subsidies and bailout money from the government, while Mercedes, BMW, Lexus, Infiniti, and Bentley are prospering. You have to study these examples carefully and learn to compete against free and low-cost products and service and prosper. Later in this book, I will tell you how I have maintained a 70 percent gross profit on my products since inception in 1975 in the presence of brutal competition and through several recessions.

The seven steps of the core business cycle are the basics of your business. Any activity performed outside of this cycle is secondary. If anything appears to go wrong in your business, go back to the basics, analyze, and find out what could be the cause of the problem and take corrective actions immediately. Have a written procedure on how to perform each of these seven steps, and have it available for everybody in your organization.

You should have a policy manual with the job description for each of your employees. When you hire your employees, train them extensively for what they will be doing as per their job description. They should have some knowledge of overall company policy, how they fit in with other employees as a team, and they should know how to perform their duties well.

Action. How you put your plan into action will determine how much success you will have as an entrepreneur.
The adjective that goes with action is *massive*. In the final analysis, you have to act. You have no control over the final results, but you have complete control over your activities with respect to the seven steps of the core business cycle. To quote Thomas Huxley, "The great end of knowledge is not knowledge, but action."

Learn how to spend your time wisely. Every night you should have a list of activities you will perform tomorrow. Grade them from the most important to least important. Start your day with the most important activity that adds value to your business. Learn to delegate work that can be done by one of your associates. If an associate can do something, you should not be doing it. Concentrate on the most important activity that only you can do. Keep cross-referencing or checking your daily list as you are making progress.

How do you take your enterprise to the next level?

As you start your enterprise, you are wearing half-dozen hats, and by doing so, you are making a good profit. You are keeping your overhead low. You can grow your gross revenue in the range of $500,000 to $1,000,000. Most entrepreneurs get stuck in this revenue range and make a good living. If that is your goal, congratulations—you made it. You should have a few loyal employees, a low-rent facility, and a few dependable customers and clients.

However, some entrepreneurs are more ambitious. They want to be recognized as icons in the business world and would like to build an industrial empire like Donald Trump, Steve Jobs, or Bill Gates. If you want to be like them, then you have to be ready to face and be prepared to overcome several challenges. These challenges are primarily in three areas:

1. *Human resources.* Hiring, training, and managing a large number of employees.

2. *Space limitation.* If your revenue is growing to over a million dollars, then you cannot operate from your home, unless you are in an Internet-related or consulting business. You have to have proper office space with phones, desks, chairs, computers, and other office equipment.

3. Paperwork blizzard. As your revenue grows, processing the orders; shipping the products; invoicing; accounts receivables; accounts payables; and city, state, and federal reporting start picking up.

Overcoming these challenges without hurting the core of the business operation separates a small business from a big business. This step is very stressful and sometimes causes the demise of the business if not done properly. It can be extremely nerve-racking. You will have to learn a lot about your operation, and you will have to make a lot of decisions that will be very important and crucial to your future and the future of your business.

As you proceed with reading this book, I will teach you how to overcome these challenges. One thing I want to tell you here is that you will have to reach out beyond yourself and learn to build a management team.

Building a management team

Whether your company has five employees or fifty, it cannot function smoothly without a chain of command. Unless yours is literally a one-man operation, division of responsibility is unavoidable. When you hire your first worker, the workload must be divided. Within a company of any size the job descriptions of each worker are not only helpful they are essential. They clearly outline for each worker where his or her responsibilities start and how they mesh with those of other workers of the team and other departments in the company.

Management is the art of getting things done through people. It takes a leadership ability on the part of the management to accomplish this. It is said that leaders do the right things and managers do the things right. How can you apply these principles in your business?

Scott A. Clark, in his book *Beating the Odds*, writes that venture capitalists weigh the success of a business plan on the following basis:

The management team: 54 percent

The industry: 24 percent

The product: 16 percent

The planning: 6 percent

Note that the management team's contribution to the success formula is almost four times greater than the product's contribution. The truth is that an experienced management team beats a dynamic product every time.

Few successful businesses are the result of one person's solo efforts. It is not enough for an entrepreneur to be good at producing a fine product or performing an excellent service. If your business is to grow, you must be a leader to get others to commit to your vision and work at making it a reality.

Different management styles for different tasks

No one management style is best for every task, every employee, and every manager. Most entrepreneurs are pragmatic. They are not sold on one management style. They judge their success by achieving their objectives. There are three well-established management styles. They are (1) autocratic, (2) democratic, and (3) management by objective. They all have advantages and disadvantages.

1. Autocratic management

Advantages

In the case of product manufacturing, assembling, and fast-food restaurants—where everything has to be done in a routine, repetitive, and precise way, and where the employees are lacking the necessary experience and motivation—autocratic management produces quality products every time with uniform composition and characteristics. This management style works very well in a fast-paced environment where there is no time to confer and consult with others. In this case, the manager makes all the decisions and gives orders rather than asking for advice. When the situation calls for fast, decisive action, the boss is ready to move on a dime and get good results on time continuously.

Disadvantages

Autocratic management creates resentment and frustration among workers who feel ignored and not part of the team. In the long run, their motivation is very low and the quality of work may suffer. This style also limits the growth of the individuals to take on more important and meaningful work in the company.

2. Democratic management

Advantages

In an operation where employees have a good education, excellent job skills, and motivation to do their work well, the democratic management style works well. The manager encourages employees to get involved in the process and delegates authority whenever possible but remains the final and financial authority on the decision-making process. This style provides the feeling of belonging, pride, and commitment to the mission of the company.

Disadvantages

It takes time to get employees' input; with the large volume of input that is sure to come, it takes away from the full meaning of the original idea and waters down the decisions that can occur in reaching the consensus.

3. Management by objective

Advantages

In the case of professionals, scientists, engineers, analysts, and outside salespeople, this style of management works well. Here, managers hire mature, skilled, and well-motivated achievers, assign them clear objectives to achieve, and then let them make most of the decisions to perform their functions and get the desired results. This management style gives employees freedom and independence to grow and fulfill the company's mission with self-satisfaction.

Disadvantages

By letting employees set their own agenda, workers can end up pursuing their own interests rather than fulfilling the company mission.

You judge your operation and analyze the functions that each employee is doing to achieve his or her tasks, and then you decide what style of management you have to utilize. Each individual employee is different. While one style works for one, it may not work for another. The first rule of management is that you inspect what you expect. Let each of your employees know what his or her assignment is. Train them to do their job well, give them authority to do their job, and then inspect the results received. Be open, honest, and clear to them when they live up to your expectations. If not, tell them what they have to do to achieve your expectations. Make it clear to employees that they can come to you for help and you will provide them the help they ask for. Set them up for success and encourage and compliment them for their achievements and for a job well done.

Motivating your employees to excel

Every individual working for you has different needs and different wants. That is the reason they come to work. The majority of employees have a need for a paycheck to pay their bills and take care of their family. But money is not the only motivator. There are other motivators, including interesting work; recognition; responsibility; new challenges; opportunity for advancement, bonuses, and trips to exotic places; good fringe benefits; job security; and flexible hours.

The word *motivation* means motive to action. The trick is to know the motivation that gets each individual to come to work. Everybody is motivated by something. The man who does not come to work because he wants to sleep that day? He is motivated all right—motivated to sleep that day! How can a manager make him believe that coming to work and being punctual on the job is better for his career and financial advancement than sleeping in? This is the big challenge for the manager. But that's what managers get paid for.

To motivate others to work for my company's mission, I have to be motivated and upbeat. I tell my associates "Do not spend too much time in bed." Most people die there. Before they die physically, they die financially. If you come to work on time and work sincerely, you will get more raises and will have job security in good times and bad.

Chris Jones was a public school student who was always causing trouble; he did not listen to his teachers, did not do his homework, fought with his classmates, and argued with authority figures. The school's principal often called Chris's father to his office to discuss the boy's latest antics. After several unpleasant exchanges with the principal and no improvement from Chris, Mr. Jones grew frustrated and put Chris in a private school that had a very low teacher-to-student ratio, which Mr. Jones thought would benefit Chris. It did—briefly. In only a few months, Chris was up to his tricks again. Once more, Mr. Jones started getting calls from the school principal, and despite lengthy lectures from his father, Chris showed no improvement. After several months, Mr. Jones put Chris in a military school that was a hundred miles away. He thought the military school's discipline and daily morning drills would fix Chris's behavioral problems, but in a matter of months it all started again. After a few weeks and many hundred-mile trips, Mr. Jones got tired and gave up any hope of Chris ever doing well. Finally, he enrolled Chris to a Catholic school that was just across the street from their home and hoped for the best. Every day Mr. Jones waited for the inevitable call about Chris's bad behavior. It never came; three months passed without so much as a note from a teacher. Mr. Jones was surprised. He called the sister who was the principal of the school and asked how Chris was doing. She said, "Chris is a model student and is very respectful of his classmates and teachers. He does his homework and submits it on time." She congratulated Mr. Jones for raising such a nice young boy. Mr. Jones thanked the sister and thought, "Sister, you do not know Chris. Just give him a few more months."

Three more months passed, and Mr. Jones did not hear from the sister. Then curiosity got the best of him, and he came home early one day to check on Chris. Chris came home from school and went straight to his room. Mr. Jones said, "Son, I want to talk to you." Chris replied that he needed to do his homework first. Mr. Jones said, "Son, I am very proud of you and of what you are doing at your school. I'll wait until you're done with your homework. Then we'll talk." After Chris finished his homework, he went to his father. Mr. Jones said, "Son, I am very pleased with your progress in school. You had so many problems in the other schools…what happened in this school that you are doing so well?" Chris replied, "When you took me to this school, I saw that man on the cross, and I knew they meant business." He had seen Jesus on the cross, and the fear of God motivated to excel in school. The manager has to decide what motivates each individual worker to excel.

We, as entrepreneurs and managers, are like battery chargers. If the battery charger is down, it cannot charge the battery. During this time of uncertainty in our economy, subprime loans, bank failures, and government bailouts, people ask me, "Doc, how can you have such high energy and enthusiasm in this recession?" I reply that I decided not to participate in this recession. To that, they laugh. The year 2008 was our best year at Chemco, and 2009 appears to have been even better. We have been hiring, training, and managing more salespeople and other employees. During this tough time, our competitors are hurting. Somebody has to supply the needed cleaning and maintenance products to our customers. That's us, and we are doing it and doing it well. In good times, anybody can be happy and excited, but it takes a good manager and an eternal optimist to be happy and excited in bad times. Good managers are steady and stay the course, knowing that good times are just around the corner. This is not the first time we have had a recession in this country. Big expansion of our economy has come every time after every recession. That is what we are excited about, and why we continue sowing the good seeds and keep doing the good deeds during the bad times. This is the way we can harvest a good crop when the good times roll back in, as they always do. There is a bright day after every dark night, and there is sunshine after every muddy and messy rainfall. Hang in there—things will change for the better.

Sam Walton's rules for building your business

Sam Walton, the legendary founder of Walmart, the largest retailer in the world, certainly knew how to build a business from scratch. He sets ten formulas for building a business, and

I want to share the essence with you. They come from his book *Sam Walton: Made in America.*

Rule 1: Commit to your business. Believe in it more than anybody. If you love your work, you will be out there every day trying to do it the best you possibly can, and pretty soon everyone around you will catch the passion from you—like a fever.

Rule 2: Share your profits with all of your associates and treat them as partners. In turn, they will treat you as a partner, and together you will all perform beyond your wildest expectations. Remain a corporation and retain control if you like, but behave as a servant-leader in a partnership.

Rule 3: Motivate your partners (employees). Money and ownership alone are not enough. Constantly, day by day, think of new and more interesting ways to motivate and challenge your partners. Keep everybody guessing as to what your next trick is going to be. Do not become too predictable.

Rule 4: Communicate everything you possibly can to your partners. The more they know, the more they will understand. The more they understand, the more they will care. Once they care, there is no stopping them.

Rule 5: Appreciate everything your associates do for the business. All of us like to be told how much somebody appreciates what we do for them. Appreciation is absolutely free— and worth a fortune.

Rule 6: Celebrate your success. Find some humor in your failures. Don't take yourself too seriously. Loosen up, and everybody around you will loosen up. Have fun. Show enthusiasm—always.

Rule 7: Listen to everyone in your company and figure out ways to get them talking. The folks on the front lines— the ones who actually talk to the customers—are the ones who really know what's going on out there.

Rule 8: Exceed your customers' expectations. If you do, they will come back over and over again. Give them what they want—and a little more. Stand behind everything you do.

Rule 9: Control your expenses better than your competition. This is where you can always find the competitive advantage.

Rule 10: Swim upstream. Go the other way. Ignore the conventional wisdom. If everybody else is doing it one way, there's a good chance you can find your niche by going in exactly the other way.

Seven ways to expand and grow your business

First you have to establish your business and make a profit. Then you develop and refine a prototype that can be multiplied. Now you are ready to expand your business as follows:

1. New Market Area: Open a new location in another part of your town, state, or country. If you have a direct sales force, open a new office manned by a manager and staff. Duplicate the same thing that you have successfully done in your original location.

2. Purchasing Your Competition: Most of the big names in business that we know today have grown by mergers and acquisitions. Xerox, IBM, GE, Boeing, AT&T, Ameren, Emerson Electric, and many companies became giants by buying their smaller and in some cases even their bigger competitors. You can do it, too. However, you should do it without overleveraging.

3. Placing Your Products on the GSA Schedule: This important option is explained step by step in chapter 6. Study and implement it, and put your business on autopilot to grow continuously, as I have done.

4. Franchising: Sell a franchise like Subway, RE/MAX Realty, and McDonald's restaurants. It is an exact copy of your successful business that can be sold as a stand-alone entity.

You receive a franchise fee and continued royalty based on the franchisee's sales.

5. Licensing Agreement: You can sell the licensing agreement to other entrepreneurs to duplicate and operate your type of business within certain agreed-upon guidelines and operating procedures. You receive royalties based on their sales.

6. Internet Marketing: This can be a very popular and profitable way to expand your business if your products and/or services can be delivered throughout the country and even the world.

7. International Marketing: Due to technological advancement and the Internet, the world is a lot smaller place than it used to be. Global marketing is another way to grow your business.

Acres of diamonds in your backyard

As you try to expand your business, my advice to you is to realize that there is an acre of diamonds in your own backyard. I tell a story about a farmer who had a small farm near Istanbul, Turkey. He was a hard worker but because of varying weather conditions, he had problem getting a good crop year after year. He then heard that there was a diamond mine in Cyprus. He sold his farm, went to Cyprus, invested his money in the search for diamonds, and ended up losing everything. He was getting old, feeble, and tired. He decided to go back to his hometown and see how things were there. He could not believe what had happened. Lights were dazzling, and new restaurants and hotels had been built not far from his old farm. He went to a coffee shop and asked a young man about the big changes in the town. The young man replied, "You wouldn't believe it. There was a farmer who sold his farm and went to Cyprus to search for diamonds. The new owner saw some glittering particles on the farm, hired a geologist who found diamonds, and the rest is history. I don't know what happened to the farmer who sold the farm." To that the old farmer replied, "I don't know either."

Do not let that happen to you. Dig deep, try hard, and become number one, two, or three in your market first before going anywhere else.

CHAPTER VI

How to Win and Keep Government Contracts

In the thirty-five years since I founded Chemco, I have learned how to build a successful business by selling to all departments of government on the local, state, and federal levels. In this chapter I will share with you the lessons I learned about how to sell to and cement professional partnership with the people in government who have the power of the purse.

Selling to city, county, and state governments without bidding

Before starting my company, I had worked for about five months as a commissioned salesperson for a chemical sales company that sold its products primarily to the different departments of cities, counties, and states. Within a few months I realized that this was a lucrative and stable market even in recessionary times. Governmental departments such as sewer and water plants; street and highway departments; fire, ambulance, and police departments; parks and recreation departments; city halls, courthouses, civic centers, and school districts all have annual budgets. Most of the time, the department heads have the authority to purchase whatever they need for their departments without going through a formal bidding process. If they like you and your products, they can purchase them right then and there. The price is important but not as important as it would be in a formal bidding process, which can be a time-consuming and inefficient way of doing business. In addition, the products purchased through such a process are not always as high quality as Chemco's products are. The department heads know that and prefer to purchase them in smaller quantities as needed. I found the following advantages by working with and selling to these departments:

a. Their departments never go out of business, and they pay their bills on time.

b. Since their department heads work with both process and equipment, they have to be present in case something goes wrong. So they are rarely "too busy," meaning a salesperson can see and sell them without setting up an appointment.

c. Since salespeople work without an appointment, they can plan to see twelve to fifteen of these department heads a day, actually meeting with five or six of them and getting two or three orders per day. You will invariably see five to six of them and get two to three orders per day. These are not huge orders, but salespeople can make a very good living if they do their job well.

d. This market is big and not limited by geographic, weather, or economic conditions. No matter what condition the economy is in, water, sewer, street, highway, fire, and police have to be budgeted and supplied. What's more, every city small or large has these departments.

e. If you can hire, train, and manage a team of outside salespeople who can take care of the customers in their defined territory, you as an entrepreneur can become wealthy.

f. If you can have field trainers and district, regional, and national sales managers who do their own hiring, training, and managing of the field sales force, your company can be a giant in its field and a very profitable enterprise.

The sales techniques described in chapter 4 are especially suited to this market. Next is how you can do business—big business—with the largest customer in the world.

Selling to the federal government with or without bidding

The U.S. government is the biggest buyer there is, spending over $500 billion or more per year. In addition to that, the fifty state governments have a combined buying power that is equal to that of the federal government. If you combine their total spending, it is nearly $1 trillion per year. No matter what you are selling—whether paper clips, rubber bands, trash bags, or complicated, high-tech gears, equipment, or cleaning products—chances are Uncle Sam is buying it.

Thousands of purchase orders and contracts worth billions of dollars bypass small businesses every year because small companies do not know of or understand the government procurement process. While dealing with the government's maze of rules and regulations can be daunting, it can also be quite lucrative. By law, 20 percent of all federal contracts are supposed to go to small businesses. Contracts in the amounts between $2,500 and $100,000 are also reserved for small businesses.

There is a lot of opportunity for small businesses to flourish in federal government contracting. If you decide to avail yourself of this opportunity, you should have the following:

a. Profitable and ongoing business.

b. Time and patience to hang in there because dealing with the government is an ordeal filled with red tape and setbacks.

c. Designated, trained personnel to do the paperwork on a daily basis.

What follows is a step-by-step approach to doing business with the U.S. government. The information is based on Business Owners' Toolkit's Small Business Guide (toolkit. com) with some modifications and on my personal experiences in doing business with the federal government in general and the General Services Administration (GSA) in particular.

You and your business are about to embark on a brand-new adventure. You will be entering a new $500-billion market in pursuit of a daunting new customer, the federal government of the United States of America. Does that sound overwhelming? Not if you understand the rules, the process, what to do, when to do it, and where to go for help.

The opportunities and ground rules

1. According to the SBA, the federal government wrote 10.3 million contracts for products and services in fiscal year 2005. In addition to these contracts, the federal government's use of credit cards resulted in another 26.5 million transactions. The 10.3 million contracts resulted in $400 billion worth of business, while the credit card transactions amounted to additional sales of $16.4 billion. Since any federal contracts in amounts between $2,500 and $100,000 are reserved for small, small disadvantaged, small women-owned, and small veteran-owned businesses, almost 10 million contracts are reserved for small businesses. The government has the following designated goals for awarding prime contracts to small businesses:

a. To small business: 23 percent

b. To small disadvantaged business: 5 percent

c. To small women-owned business: 5 percent

d. To hub zone small business: 3 percent

e. To small veteran-owned business: 3 percent

2. *Government purchasing thresholds*
   a. Micro purchases (credit cards): for contracts up to $3,000
   b. Simplified Acquisition Procedures (SAP): for contracts $3,001 to $100,000
   c. Simplified commercial contracts: $100,000 to $5,000,000
   d. Commercial Off-the-Shelf (COTS), any dollar size contract (no dollar limit).
   e. Commercial items: for contracts over $3,000
   f. Sealed bids/negotiations: FAR (Federal Acquisition Regulation) parts 14815 apply for contracts $100,000 and up.

3. *Know the GSA (General Services Administration).* If your company produces or provides an item or service that is commercial or general purpose in nature, there is a good chance you will be selling to the General Services Administration (GSA) rather than to individual government offices. The GSA buys for all departments of the federal government and each department of the military and the civilian government buys products and services from GSA. Such products and services include furniture, cleaning supplies, paints, copiers, hardware, appliances, pest control, financial information technology, training, and travel services. If these are the types of products or services you sell, be sure to get in contact with the GSA office nearest you.

The GSA is one of the government's largest agencies. It helps other agencies acquire the products, services, real estate, and vehicles they need from federal and commercial sources. It acts as a catalyst for over $100 billion in federal spending annually, an amount which accounts for over 25 percent of the U.S. government's total procurement outlay. The GSA simplifies government buying and reduces government costs by negotiating large multiuser contracts and by leveraging the volume of the federal market to drive down prices. Federal agencies then place orders against these contracts. GSA contracts are awarded for a period of five years with three- to five-year option clauses. Most GSA contracts are for standard types of services and commercial off-the-shelf (COTS) products and equipment in three major areas:

a. General-purpose supplies, equipment, vehicles, and services

b. Office space and land management, building construction, repair, and maintenance

c. Information technology (IT) and professional services

GSA contracts are available to large and small businesses for local and nationwide services. All GSA contracts over $25,000 are advertised at the fedbizopps.com Web site.

If your company provides commercial products or services, the GSA is your potential customer. The GSA has two service organizations:

a. *Public Building Service (PBS).* PBS maintains multimillions of square feet of workspace for millions of federal employees all over the country. PBS owns these properties or leases them from businesses large and small.

b. *Federal Acquisition Services (FAS):* FAS provides federal and other customers with the products, services, and programs they need to meet their supply, service, procurement, vehicle purchasing and leasing, travel and transportation contracts, and property management services.

Since the GSA Office of Commercial Acquisition presents the greatest opportunity for small businesses, we will discuss this agency in detail to get you started in this very lucrative niche market.

How to get on the GSA schedule
1. Registration

Register your company on the Central Contractor Registration (CCR) at ccr.gov. This is the main database of all the suppliers of products and services that are doing business with the federal government. Go to ccr.gov and enter the required information about your company. If you have questions, call 1-866-606-8220 for assistance. To complete the CCR registration, you must provide the following:

a. DUNS number. You receive your DUNS (Data Universal Numbering System) from the Dunn & Bradstreet Company (D&B). Call D&B at 1-866-705-5711 and tell them the name, address, phone number of your company, date founded, and type of business. You can also go to D&B's Web site (dnb.com) and request a DUNS number there. You should receive your unique nine-digit number within a week.

b. CAGE code. If you do not have the Commercial and Government Entity (CAGE) code, you can submit the CCR registration without it. You will be provided your code, a five-character identification number, as a part of the CCR registration process. The CAGE code, distributed by the U.S. Department of Defense, is to identify specific companies like yours.

c. FEIN number. The federal employment identification number, also known as the tax identification number (TIN), is a nine-digit number that your company needs for income tax purposes. You can use your Social Security number if your business is not incorporated. If you need the FEIN number, you can receive one by calling the Internal Revenue Service at 1-800-829-1040. Fill in the nine-digit FEIN number (without hyphens) on the CCR registration form.

In addition to these numbers, you will need the following classification codes:

a. NAICS codes. North American Industry Classification System codes are used for classifying businesses and industries doing business with the government. If you do not have your NAICS codes, you can search the Internet at census. gov for links to NAICS search site. Go to the site and click on the NAICS in the "Business and Industry" category. Click on "Product Classification" on the top bar and then click on the 2007 numerical list. Select the category that best describes your product. If you provide services, click on "Service Sectors (NAPCS)." Get more than one NAICS code and fill them in on the CCR registration form. For Chemco, I clicked 325 Chemical Manufacturing and I found the following:

421 325 6125—Specialty cleaning and sanitation products

422 325 125111—Disinfectants—non agricultural

428 325 6125421—Glass window cleaner

431 325 6125441—Oven cleaner

b. SIC codes. The government to classify businesses and industries issues standard Industrial Classification codes. Even SIC codes are not used as much; it is still a mandatory field in the CCR registration. If you do not know your SIC codes, you can search them on the Internet at osha.gov. Click on "Statistics in Programs and Resources." Click on "SIC Manual." For Chemco, it is major group 28: Chemicals and Allied Products. For Chemco, it is as follows:

2841: Soap and other detergents

2842: Specialty cleaning, polishing, and sanitation preparations

You will find the SIC code for your products and services.

You now have most of the information to complete the CCR registration. Click on "Start New Registration" on the top left of the CCR Web site and follow the information requested. Submit it after you are satisfied that all the information is correct to the best of your knowledge. You will get the confirmation of your registration in a few days.

1. Find out the specific GSA schedule and specific special item number (SIN) that apply to your products and services

Currently, there are more than forty schedules available for the Multiple Award Schedule (MAS). In order to find which one applies to your business, search for it on the Internet at gsaadvantage.gov. Click on "Schedules e-Library." Enter the keyword that describes your business. For Chemco, I would enter "Cleaning and Polishing Preparations." I find that my products schedule number is 073 and my SIN category is 375 363 Cleaner/Degreasers. You can find your own schedule number and SIN category the same way I did.

Now click on the highlighted SIN category. You will get the complete list of current supplies for that category. They are your competitors against whom you will compete after your products are on the GSA schedule. Learn about them. You will get your competitors' Web sites, phone numbers, e-mail addresses, their contract numbers, and socioeconomic status— small business (es), women-owned (w), disadvantaged (dv), or 8a or veteran-owned (v). Mark this as a favorite and study the list.

2. Learning and researching your competitors

Visit the GSA e-library page, where you can see a list of your competitors and find what they are offering and at what price. If you are on the schedule 073 and SIN 375 363 category, click on my company, Chemco Industries, Inc. You will see that Chemco has twenty-one special item numbers (SIN) on that schedule. If you were to compete against Chemco, click on the highlighted SIN 375-117. Now you see how many other companies you will be competing against.

Next go to gsaadvantage.gov and enter "Chemco Industries, Inc." at the top left, where you see "Enter Keywords." Click on "Find it." You will see that Chemco has 1,473 products on the GSA multiple-award schedule with the negotiated price for each. This is valuable information that you can use to price your products competitively. This entry also shows the different packaging for each product that Chemco offers.

Next you should conduct further research to know what sales volume each of your competitors is making with the different agencies of the federal government and which agencies are buying most of these products so that you can concentrate your marketing efforts with those agencies with those products.

To find this information, go to fpds.gov and click on "Register" since you are not registered as of yet. Click on the second blue sentence, "Click here to establish an account," which will allow you to create account reports and retrieve data. Scroll to the bottom of the page and click on "Yes." Fill out the short application. Be sure to read and follow "User ID and Password Restrictions" by clicking on it. This shows that the user ID must be a minimum of six characters. Your user ID password must be a minimum of eight characters that should include characters, numbers, and special characters like @, _, -, and. After completing the application, click on "Save." Now log onto 4GSRI.com and click on "Small Business Resource" on the left side of the screen. Scroll down until you see "FPDS-NG" and click on it once (it is the fourth heading, in blue). A new screen will appear; log in with your login number and password. It will bring you to the EZ-Search screen. Click on the button that says, "Standard Reports" (it is the second one on the top). Click on the box on top that says "What." On the next screen, click once on "Contract Detail Report." Then, on the following screen, enter the competitor's GSA contract number (without dashes) in the box next to where it says "PIID" and hit "Execute." A list will pop up showing the GSA orders that this company received, the agencies that placed the orders, and the names of the purchasing agents. Match the "contracting agency ID" on the customer list with the "agency code" on the database.

3. Download the solicitation package and follow these directions

a. Go to fedbizopps.com.

b. Click on "Advance Search" at the top left of the page and click "Go" to find the "Find Business Opportunities" page.

c. Enter your schedule number in the "Full Text Search" space—scroll down to "Search by Agency," highlight "General Services Administration" and click the "Start Search" button at the bottom of the page.

d. Download all documents, including the solicitation and modifications, and follow the instructions to complete them.

4. Complete the solicitation package as directed

Read and understand all the forms, modifications, and required documents such as your catalogue and price list. Contact your contracting officer with any questions you might have. GSA receives a fee of 0.75 percent of your quarterly sales, so the contracting officer has a genuine interest in having you as one of his vendors. These officers are very cooperative and helpful. Mail the completed package to the contracting officer.

5. *Get on the GSA schedule*

Once the contracting officer receives your package, the officer will review it and call you to resolve any discrepancies and negotiate the best price and a prompt-payment discount. Chemco gives them net thirty days, but no discount. We also give them FOB origin, which means GSA pays the freight charges from our dock in most cases, unless an individual order is negotiated for free freight in advance. We provide domestic delivery only.

A few weeks after the final negotiation, you will receive the approval package to log onto the GSA Web site for the final approval and publication at the gsaadvantage.gov.

Congratulations!

Now you are ready to do business with all branches of the federal government. If you need more information about how to get on a GSA schedule, the GSA recommends taking the self-paced training course "How to Become a Contractor—GSA Schedule Program," which includes:

    a. various features of the GSA Schedule Program;

    b. ways to submit an offer;

    c. a look at the evaluation and contract award processes;

    d. the successful marketing of your products and/or services;

    e. sources of information related to Schedule Contract Administrations

    This course is available on the Web site of the Center for Acquisition Excellence at http://gsa.gov/cae

6. Marketing your products/services to GSA customers

Being a GSA schedule contractor is hard work. You have done that and your products are now on the www.gsaadvantage.gov Web page available for GSA buyers to purchase. Your products are approved, their prices negotiated and published. Your GSA schedule is a hunting license that allows you to pursue federal businesses and opportunities. However, without proper marketing, you will not receive many orders. Following these steps will help you market your company to all the federal agencies that need and purchase your type of products/services.

a. Prepare your electronic product catalogue and submit it to GSA Advantage by using the Schedule Input Program (SIP) software available by download at the GSA Vendor Support Center (VSC) Web site. Register at the VSC Web site and get a password. The VSC staff is to assist you with the submission. You can reach staff members by calling 877-495-4849. To see how it's done, visit the Chemco Web site, www.chemcocorp-gsa.com. Be sure to have a detailed product description stating function and using action words. Buying customers will not know your product name, such as Chemco Wasp-Away. Instead they will conduct a generic search for wasp and hornet killer. So have it "Wasp and Hornet Killer" *Wasp-Away*. Have nice pictures of your product to attract customers' attention.

b. Make your company Web site *GSA-customer friendly*. Use the GSA logo on your company Web page. Provide a link from your company's Web site to your product listing on the GSA Advantage site.

c. Market your GSA schedule contract to any and all federal agencies in your area that might use your products, including Air Force, Navy, and Army bases, the postal service, VA hospitals and national cemeteries, federal courthouses, the U.S. Army Corps of Engineers, National Guard facilities, and federal prisons. Visit the buyers for these facilities personally. Learn their buying habits and schedule, and use that information and experience to market your product/service nationwide.

d. The federal government's fiscal year starts on October 1 and ends on September 30. This means that during the months of August and September, 30 to 40 percent of the purchases are made. Capitalize on this marketing opportunity.

e. During the months of August and September, run year-end sales and special lower pricing to attract new buyers and build new sales relationships. Temporary price reductions are reviewed very quickly and are posted to gsaadvantage.gov within a day or two. Items on sale are flagged on gsaadvantage.gov with a *Sale* icon and thus will attract more attention to your products.

f. Distinguish your company and products from the competition. The government mandates that a certain percentage of procurement dollars must go to small businesses, women-owned small businesses, minority-owned small businesses, disabled-veteran-owned small businesses, or 8(a) certified minority businesses. When buyers search for a particular product, they can sort and filter results by these categories. If you qualify for these privileges, make sure your site is highlighted for these added benefits.

g. Update your Web page on the GSA Advantage site frequently with your new products, updated prices, and fresh pictures, and keep contact information up to date so that buyers can reach you as needed.

h. It is important to be proactive in reaching out to your customers on a regular basis by e-mail, phone, and special promotions. If you have established close relationships with a buyer or an agency, contact that person to capitalize on fiscal year-end spending and to close some sales. Customer relationships are critical in any sales environment and are even more so in government sales. So find ways and reasons to reach buyers on a regular basis. If you think getting on the GSA schedule and doing business with the federal government is difficult, I have a question for you, "Do you know any easy way to make serious money?" If you do, let me know. There is none. But if you follow the above advice and directions, you will enjoy a continuous stream of revenue while you are developing your core business with your regular customers. By obtaining the GSA schedule contract, you put your business on autopilot for growth.

CHAPTER VII

How to Select Professional Services

Most entrepreneurs are very confident of their abilities and are proud of their game plan to achieve their goals. However, they do not know everything, and, smart businesspeople that they are, they are the first to realize this. They are wise enough to know that they need help from experts outside their business. It is not good business to play a game when you don't know the rules and cannot understand the procedures. The fields of law, accounting, taxes, banking, advertising, and managing are such games. You need to find those professionals who can play with you and for you when the game gets under way. Your biggest challenge is to find the right players. This chapter will clarify and assist you in doing so.

Lawyer

When I started Chemco in 1975, I asked my insurance agent whether he knew an attorney who could help me incorporate my company. He recommended an attorney who was also a CPA (certified public accountant). I contacted the attorney-CPA and set up an appointment at his office about my new business. When I arrived, I found that he was the owner of a rather sizeable law and accounting firm bearing his name. His offices occupied a half floor twelve stories up in a large building in the financial district. I was impressed when I entered his private corner office. I could see almost the entire city in the panoramic twelfth-floor view. And I knew at once the man's services would not come cheap—and they didn't, even though his associates did all the paperwork for the incorporation filing. I, not knowing any better, also hired his firm to do my accounting work, which I later discovered was a mistake.

Fee building

During the beginning years at Chemco, I was very careful with my expenses. Then I started receiving bills for my gold-plated legal services. As I said, a young associate of the lawyer did most of the initial work. The charges for his time were more than twice the hourly wage I could charge for my time, and I had ten years of college, which was at least three more years than the associate! I started questioning these bills, especially for the time spent on research, and asked the firm to itemize its bills. To make matters worse the firm's accountant had some personal problems and would not get my taxes filed on time, always filing for extensions. Naturally the time spent on extension filings was billed to me, and I became increasingly disturbed about the firm's services and fees.

How to find a good attorney who will fight for you

I learned that in most metropolitan cities and communities, there is a free service called Lawyer Referral and Information Service sponsored by the bar association of that jurisdiction. After learning of this service, I set up an appointment with one of their lawyers for a token fee ($3 at that time, now available at abanet.org/legal services). The lawyer listened to my legal problems and gave me the names of three lawyers whom I could interview for thirty minutes for no charge. After that I could hire the one with whom I felt most comfortable. This was very valuable information. Most of the referred lawyers were young and were facing similar start-up challenges at that stage of their professional careers as I was. I got along very well with one of them and hired him. He was my lawyer for a long time. Later, his firm merged with another firm; still later he formed his own law firm. Every time he changed allegiance, his fees got higher and higher for the same work he had done before. Then he started assigning my work to his younger associates, and some of them were just out of law school. I always wondered who in his right mind would pay those absurdly high hourly charges for such inexperienced young lawyers. The fees of lawyers at this time are similar to what doctors were charging in the 1970s and 1980s. There is no control on their fees. Most lawyers are more negative than positive. In reality, they are frequently poor at business. Lawyers are naturally aggressive nitpickers and fog finders, have a profound superiority complex (second only to that of doctors), and always look for more money in any way they can. Unfortunately, they are a necessary evil for your enterprise. When you are suspicious of their charges, it's time to look for another tiger. That is what I did, and I found one who was not a big one but big enough to fill my needs and not too much of a man-eater to charge me ridiculously high fees.

What your lawyer can do for you

Your attorney has two primary duties: defend you when you are in trouble and attack your adversaries vigorously without mercy. You need a lawyer who can fight for you. If he or she is acting like an impartial judge rather than an advocate, look for another lawyer. You will have no trouble finding one because there is an oversupply of lawyers throughout the country. Here is what a good lawyer can do for you:

    a.   He can tell you when to sign and when not to sign contracts and agreements.

    b.   He can draw up agreements for you and have people sign those that are lopsidedly written in your favor.

    c.   He can get any number of harassing bureaucrats and complainers off your back.

    d.   He can force settlements that you would be otherwise unable to make.

    e.   He can collect money for you from hard-to-collect people.

    f.   He can help you set up deals that will be beneficial to you.

    g.   He can get you out of civil or criminal trouble.

    h.   He can help you save as well as make a lot of money.

How to get the most out of your money

When you meet your new attorney, be certain both of you put all your cards on the table. Have the lawyer tell you clearly what will be his hourly charges and what portions of his service will cost you. Do not call him up on the phone and expect free advice. Be very discreet and to the point because his clock is running. If you are about to do something new—sign a contract, purchase a building, or buy a business—contact him first. Let him describe the potential pitfalls. You may decide the game is not worth the candles. Never lose sight of the fact that the lawyer is working for you, and you do not have to abide by his advice, but at least you will be prepared for adversity if it comes your way.

Accountant

As I mentioned earlier, my original attorney was also an accountant, and I was not happy with that arrangement. Once when I was attending a bank party, an accountant approached me. He owned an accounting firm that employed three CPAs. He appeared to be very knowledgeable. Adding to the appeal was the fact that he did my bank's accounting work. I hired him. I have been with the same accounting firm for over twenty-four years. Three years ago, a large multistate firm acquired the firm. Soon I noticed their charges went up tremendously. Last year I interviewed three CPAs and hired one. He owns his accounting firm, employing three other CPAs. He has been doing excellent work and his charges are reasonable. Over the years, I have found that, unlike lawyers, most accountants are laid-back and nonaggressive. Furthermore, accountants tend to be vague in discussing fees they charge for staff accountants, senior accountants, and partners. If possible, it would be to your advantage to get those rates in writing.

Once you hire an accountant, that person will set up the chart of accounts and an accounting system for you. You should follow it without question. For the best results, you and your accountant should work together, supplying each other with accurate and timely figures. Whether your accountant handles all your record-keeping tasks or just does your taxes, it is vital that you understand what is being done. You will discover what kind of money you are making in your business and what you have to do to make more.

Consultants

Over the course of owning and operating Chemco for thirty-five years, I have tried to use several consultants specializing in small-business management, sales and marketing, financial management, and public relations. I have been disappointed every time. These men and women can talk well and write well but cannot perform to bring the needed results. Victor Kiam, in his book *Going for It*, put it best: "Consultants are like castrated bulls, and all they can do is advise." Most of them will listen to your problems, go home, and write a fancy report with everything you told them. Of course, this report comes with a big bill attached.

Hindsight is always twenty-twenty. After my unsatisfactory experience with consultants, I would only hire them again if they had an actual and successful working experience in the specialty chemical industry. Ideas are a dime a dozen, and most of the time they can't or shouldn't be implemented—mark my words. Any consultant who promises to show you how to improve your business will end up doing nothing more than wasting your time. What's more, you will be paying him to teach your business to you on the basis of information you provided him. Save your money and sanity and use your banker, lawyer, and accountant to help solve your business problems. General Colin Powell wrote, "Don't be buffaloed by experts and elites. Experts often possess more data than judgment. Elites can become so inbred that they produce hemophiliacs who bleed to death as soon as they are nicked by the real world." With all of that said, there two exceptions. They are as follows:

1. A consultant who has worked in or owned a business just like yours. He or she has inside information that you can use and implement immediately to propel your business to the next level.

2. SCORE (Service Corps of Retired Executives)

SCORE, part of the Small Business Administration (SBA), maintains a roster of retired business executives who volunteer to help entrepreneurs who need help in starting a business or solving problems in operating their current business. In my experience, SCORE offers the most important service that SBA provides. SCORE provides free, impartial, and mature counseling.

In order to receive this service, call a SCORE office near you. You will be mailed or faxed a form to complete and return. A counselor will be assigned to you to help you solve your specific problems. In my first year at Chemco, I was very fortunate to get a counselor, George Donald, who had started working for a condensed milk company as a salesman, and as the company grew and was acquired by a larger company, he received numerous promotions. Mr. Donald retired as a vice president of a large national corporation. He knew the problems of small and start-up firms first hand. Because he was an older gentleman and I had a heavy accent, I would have to explain my problems to Mr. Donald several times, but once he understood what I was saying, he had the right solutions for me. He was very kind and generous with his time and advice. Mr. Donald became a long-term mentor to me. Even though SCORE requires its counselors to be one-time problem solvers and only work with a client on a temporary basis, Mr. Donald advised me for years on his own time. SCORE is a great source of help for starting entrepreneurs, and I recommend its use highly.

Insurance agents

A reliable and qualified insurance agent is an important member of your team. To find the right agent, talk to your attorney, accountant, and business friends, and ask them to provide you with names of potential hires. Call at least three of them and invite them to your place of business. Make sure that they are commercial property/casualty underwriters (CPCU) and members of the Independent Insurance Agents of America (IIAA).

Ask for their references. Check the references to find out how good the agent is and how the insurance companies that he represents pay claims. Your insurance agent is the person in whom you are going to put your trust for the financial safety of your business. Once you find a well-qualified, trustworthy, and experienced agent, tell him what business you are in and what type of exposure you, your products, or services may have. Let him get quotes for product liability insurance, health insurance, key-man insurance, workman's compensation, building and plant insurance, and umbrella insurance. Decide whom to hire on the basis of his quotes and what you and your company can afford.

Ray Kroc, the founder of the McDonald's restaurant chain, put it this way:

"You are only as good as the people you hire."

CHAPTER VIII

How to Tame the Bureaucratic Bulls

Entrepreneurs and small businesses have three adversaries: big businesses, union bosses, and government bureaucrats. In this chapter, we will discuss the last one, bureaucrats employed by our own government—city, state, and federal. Bureaucrats seem to believe that all businesses, be they large or small, are their adversaries. They act as if most businesses violate the law, pollute the environment, and cheat on their taxes, and believe it is their divine right to protect the public and keep businesspeople in line. Because of these false assumptions, these men and women become arrogant and sometimes go beyond the spirit and even letter of the law in pressing their agenda. They harass the very people who pay most of their salary. A vast army of bureaucrats armed with paper clubs is swarming over our nation with a dedicated goal of beating the small businesses to their knees. In 1996, over seven thousand new bureaucratic regulations came out of Washington, D.C., alone. If you added up all the bureaucratic edicts coming from all the governmental agencies in America—cities, counties, and states—the amount would come to an astounding fifty thousand new regulations introduced each and every year. Most of the victims of this army of hyper-regulators are the entrepreneurs and small-business owners who have few options to fight against those harassments and intimidations levied by those bureaucratic bulls.

I had to figure out from the beginning how to handle and tame these bulls, who used to come charging in very frequently to my place of business. In this chapter, I will tell you some of the techniques that will make you victorious in taming these out-of-control bulls and marauders. In order to fight and tame them, you have to know and be sure of two things:

1. *You are on safe and firm ground.* You know that you are running your business as an ethical, law-abiding, and solid citizen.
2. *You know your rights.* As a citizen of the United States, you should know the following:
   a. *No one can search your premises or seize your property without a warrant.* Only when presented with a warrant you are required to yield your premises or property. Do not let the threat of a warrant scare you, as the court not easily or quickly authorizes warrants.
   b. *The Fifth Amendment gives you the right against self-incrimination.* The Fifth Amendment guarantees "that no person shall be compelled in any criminal case to be witness against himself." Protected by the Constitution, you do not have to give up any records if you have any trace of doubt that an inspection or audit of them will adversely affect you.
   c. *You have a right to get advance notice of an inspection or audit.* If an agent appears without an appointment and

demands to conduct his inquiry, inspection, or audit on your premise, you have the right to refuse the agent access.

d. *You have the right to be treated decently and objectively by an agent of any and all local state and federal agencies.* Since you are a taxpayer, part of your taxes pays agents' salary. Therefore, you do not have to accept any threat or abuse from these agents. They are public servants, and they are the servants and you are the public. They work for you not the other way around.

These four rights have served me well over thirty-four years that I have owned my business.

Local fire department

In 1978, I purchased a thirteen-thousand-square-foot building to use as Chemco's office, warehouse, and manufacturing facility. I then put up my company sign in front of the building. It appears that two firemen on a huge fire truck coming back from a fire saw my large sign and decided to make an unannounced inspection. My wife and the company secretary were in our office area at the time. The firefighters told them they were there to inspect the facilities. My wife told them that since the boss was not in, they needed to call and set up an appointment. She told them that he did not like anybody going through the facilities without him being present. Two men then tried to push their way past the women to do the inspection right then and there, but the ladies persisted and finally succeeded in denying them entry, after which they got very upset and left the building. When they closed the front door, they closed it so hard that it shook the entire building. When I returned to the office later, my wife told me about the unpleasant incident. I called the fire chief and told him in no uncertain terms that his firemen were on my premises without my permission and harassing my employees. I told him that as taxpayers, we had hired him and his staff to protect us, not to harm our property or us. The chief respected my opinion and set up an appointment to inspect Chemco facility, whereupon the inspectors found not a single violation. Since that time, the fire inspectors set up an appointment with me every year, inspect my facilities, and have never found a violation of any consequence. If they find any minor violation, I correct it within the specified time. After that incident in 1978, city inspectors and Chemco have gotten along.

State sales tax audit

In 1984, I got a notice from the Missouri sales tax office announcing that my company would be audited for the previous three years. Auditors gave us a list of the records, paperwork, and sales tax returns that they would require us to make available for them to audit. Two Missouri state auditors came at the appointed time. I had all the paperwork on a table in the Chemco conference room. I told my employees not to talk to the auditors. I greeted the auditors when they came in, showed them the conference room, and told them if they needed any more records, they should prepare a list in writing and give it to me. They were at Chemco eight hours a day for an entire week but said that they needed still more time to finish the audit. With that, I let them know that they were taking too much time, and if they could not complete their work that week, I would start charging them rent for my conference room. Whether or not my threat had an effect, the auditor did finish their work that week and later came in with a delinquent charge in my sales tax return for three years. It was in the amount of less than $200. I paid it but wondered how a pair of auditors could work for two weeks of taxpayers' money in my office and end up with only $200 to show for it.

OSHA inspection

Once in the mid-1990s, there was supposed to have been a conference of OSHA (the Occupational Safety and Health Administration) in St. Louis. For some reason, that conference was cancelled. It appears that the OSHA inspectors were looking for some work to justify their trip from Kansas City to St. Louis and tried to find some companies to inspect. Chemco, being a chemical company and listed high in the Yellow Pages, was picked to be inspected, which explains why, one day, two inspectors walked into our office unannounced, showed their badges like a gun to our receptionist, produced their business cards, and told her that they were there for an OSHA inspection. My receptionist, somewhat undone, came to my office, gave me their cards, and told me why the men were there. I did not want them to inspect my premises at that time, as I knew my plant was not ready for them. Most manufacturing plants, especially cleaning product manufacturers, are like your kitchen. If you are in the process of cooking, you have all of your utensils, food materials, and other things lying around. You do not want your guests to walk into your kitchen, let alone your uninvited guests such as OSHA inspectors.

Since they didn't have an appointment with me, I let the inspectors wait for over twenty minutes. Then I walked into the reception area. I said, "How may I help you? You have to hurry up since I am very busy today." They explained that they were there for a field audit. I acted very surprised and said, "I never received the prior notice of this inspection that I am entitled to." One of them claimed they had the right to conduct an inspection unannounced. I raised my voice and said, "You do not! This is not Walmart; you cannot walk in just any time. Get out of my place right now and set up an appointment for an inspection. I certainly do want you to come back because I want you to check my plant out. I work here, my wife works here, sometimes even my children work here. I don't want it to be an unsafe place to work." They made it clear they did not like my attitude, but they left the premises, presumably to spend time with someone more cooperative.

Why our high-paying manufacturing jobs are going overseas and how to reverse this trend

Our great country is not a profitable place for a low-tech manufacturer. Some of the obvious reasons are as explained above, and more reasons follow.

a. Overregulation of manufacturing practices

Manufacturing, by nature, is not always clean and safe. On September 30, 2009, the president of the Federal Reserve Bank of St. Louis invited me for the Manufacturer and International Executives Luncheon Meeting. There were dozens of local manufacturers, exporters, there and us. We were given a few minutes each to talk about why we are losing manufacturers and high paying manufacturing jobs. Almost all of us had similar bad experiences with the sudden and repeated visits and inspections by OSHA, fire departments, sewer districts, and a host of other regulators.

b. High Taxation

Every year small businesses have to pay high taxes on their inventory of raw materials, products in the process of manufacturing, and finished goods not sold. But large companies employ lobbyists who get them the variances from state and city governments so that, for example, they don't have to pay any inventory taxes.

c. Litigation

This results in high product liability insurance premiums.

Manufacturers can easily be sued for a small defect in their products, even many, many years after production. Juries in most cases award judgments in the millions to plaintiffs. These awards raise insurance premiums so high that most small manufacturers cannot afford to pay and run their business without coverage, exposing themselves to bankruptcy if sued.

d. Education or lack of it

Most manufactures employ plant workers who are primarily high school graduates or those who have obtained GED certificates. These employees require lengthy training and close supervision because of their lack of basic education.

e. High wages

Most low-tech products like shoes, clothing, phones, televisions, fans, air conditioners, toys, motors, and engines, which are manufactured by American workers, have become too expensive for even American consumers to buy.

f. Negative attitude of Americans toward American manufacturers

Americans like to make high wages but like to purchase cheap products. They do not care whether that cheap product is made here or somewhere else. Is it any wonder that American manufacturers are going away, building plants, and opening offices in Mexico, China, India, Sri Lanka, Malaysia, and other countries? In those countries, employers are not harassed on a daily basis like here. Besides, they can and do make higher profits by having their facilities there. Their workers are thankful that these companies provide them the jobs and wages to raise their families better than those who do not have jobs.

You cannot have high employment and also despise the employers. No goose means no eggs. Our government deludes itself when it imagines that it can raise employment in this country by taxing, regulating, and harassing the employers, especially manufacturers. Employers locate where they are welcomed. In order to create high-paying jobs in our country, we have to create a business environment that is conducive to employers, particularly in the manufacturing sector. Excessive regulations, high taxation, and frivolous litigation triangulate our economy and cause job migration out of our country.

g. Free market economy vs. centrally controlled economy

After World War II, in 1946, Germany was divided into two parts—East Germany and West Germany. Both parts of Germany had the same hardworking and well-educated Germans living in them. But they had two systems of governance–Communist, with its top-down central planning and autocratic, Soviet-style administration in the East, and capitalist, with a bottom-up free-enterprise system, in the West. The economy of East Germany deteriorated rapidly under Communist rule. The East Germans got tired of being underfed and overcontrolled to a point that they started to cross the border to West Germany in droves for a better life.

In 1960, the Communist government of East Germany, with the help of the Russians, built the Berlin Wall, manned by the East German army with guns and bullets to control the population from fleeing to West Germany. This state of affairs continued until 1990, when the two halves of Germany were united. During this period of forty-four years, the income per capita of West Germans was eighteen times higher than that of East Germans, proving the superiority of the free enterprise system and free market economy over the centrally controlled market under communist system.

The same experiment has been repeated in the Korean peninsula. After the Korean War, in 1953, Korea was divided in two. North Korea started under the Communist rule and centrally controlled economy, and South Korea under the capitalist form of government and free market economy. In 2008, fifty-five years later, the average income per capita in North Korea was $1,700, while in South Korea it was $26,000. North Koreans and South Koreans are the same people, with the same culture and work habits. However, under the free market economy in the South, people made over fifteen times more income than the same people in the North under a centrally controlled economy. Besides the vast difference in their income, South Koreans on average are eight inches taller than their counterparts in the North.

It does not take a rocket scientist to figure out which system of governance is better for human being. I do not know how we can convince our politicians and government bureaucrats to let the free market and capitalist system work freely to uplift our lives, our income, our employment, our educational system, and even our health care system for the better.

Winston Churchill was right when he said "The inherent vice of capitalism is the unequal sharing of blessings; the inherent virtue of socialism is the equal sharing of miseries.

The endeavor to convert American Eagles into European PIGS

Some otherwise well intentioned American politicians try to convert our free enterprise system (American eagles) that has done so much for so many for so long in this country and around the world into western European countries like Portugal, Italy, Greece, and Spain (PIGS), which have experienced extreme destruction of their financial and social structures due to their experimentation with socialism and centrally controlled governance, and are at the verge of bankruptcy. Knowing what has happened to pigs, proud and independent-minded eagles are resisting that cruel conversion and presumably good doer politicians are having ton of trouble in doing so.

That reminds me of a Boy Scout who was half an hour late for a Boy Scout meeting. The Scout master was very upset and asked the Boy Scout in a no nonsense voice, "Son, the first rule of scouting is to be punctual. Why you are late?" The Boy Scout answered, "Sir, I stopped to do a good deed on my way to the meeting." The Boy Scout master, happy with that response, said "Son, tell everybody about your good deed." The Boy Scout said with a great pride, "I helped an old lady cross the street." The Scoutmaster said, "I am very proud of what you did, but surely it didn't take you half an hour to help an old lady across the street?" To that, Boy Scout said, "Sir, I had a bit of trouble performing my good deed." "Trouble? What sort of trouble?" the Scoutmaster asked. The Boy Scout answered, "That old lady did not want to cross the street." Somebody rightly said, "If you are selling dog food, you better make sure that dog likes to eat it."

An American Success Story

My brother Bhupi was not doing well in India. He had only a high school education, was married with two sons, and did not have a steady job. Because of his precarious position, I sponsored him to come to America. My wife traveled to India to visit and brought Bhupi to St. Louis in 1985. Bhupi knew only a few words of English. He lived with my family and worked in my plant for five years. During that period, he learned English, got his driver's license, and started working part-time at Hardee's after his eight-hour day at Chemco. Eventually, he was able to bring his wife and two sons from India to St. Louis. He got promoted at Hardee's and moved to Kankakee, Illinois. A few years after moving there he was diagnosed with Parkinson's disease and could no longer work at Hardee's. At that point, Bhupi decided to go into the motel business. With my initial financial help, which he later paid me back in full, Bhupi bought his first motel, in Centralia, Illinois. He and his hard-working wife, Rita, learned the business well and bought a second motel in Carlyle, Illinois, and a third motel in Mattoon, Illinois. They were attentive parents, and their sons, Rahul and Rohit, did well in school and college. Rahul, with a master's degree in information technology, is an IT professional at a large corporation, and Rohit is currently in his second year of medical school. Rahul has found a girlfriend with a degree in economics; Rohit's girlfriend is a classmate at his medical school. My brother, his Parkinson's disease notwithstanding, and his wife, Rita, are doing very well financially. It is not only the money, but the quality of their lives that has changed for the better. Bhupi and Rita as well as Rahul's girlfriend joined us at our last Thanksgiving dinner. This generational change—from generational poverty to generational prosperity—can happen only in America. I always wonder, what would have happened to Bhupi, Rita, Rahul, and Rohit if they were still in India? My wife and I love this great American success story, and we are very proud that we had something to do with it.

CHAPTER IX

How to Formulate and Execute Your Succession Plan and Exit Strategy

Privately owned family businesses account for over 80 percent of all businesses and employ over 50 percent of the working population of the United States. Family businesses are the fastest-growing segment of our economy and create a higher percentage of employment than big businesses in good and bad economic times. According to independent sources, only about 30 percent of family businesses survive the transition to the second generation, and only 10 percent survive to the third generation. A primary reason for these unfortunate statistics is that most business owners have committed their life's work to building a successful company, but only a relatively small percentage of owners take the time and make the effort necessary to fully prepare a succession plan or exit strategy for their company.

The succession plan and exit strategy can be seen as two sides of the same coin and can be described as follows:

Succession plan

This is a legal method to transfer the control of a business to family members or to existing and related shareholders, such as your spouse, child or children, or business partner(s). A succession plan is what is called an inside transfer of power, control, and management of a business.

Exit strategy

This is a method of selling a business to an outside entity through the following processes:

A. Taking the business public (IPO: initial public offering)
B. Selling the business to your employees (ESOP: employee stock ownership plan)
C. Selling the business in the open market
D. Bankruptcy filing, either Chapter 11 or Chapter 7
E. Closing the door and walking out

For an entrepreneur who starts his own business and has some success, his business becomes the most important thing in his life. This psychological attachment, in most cases, deters him from planning for the succession of or exit from the business, which can become a difficult and emotional issue for him.

Let me give you an example of a succession plan that looked perfect but, in the end, lacked a key ingredient: desire on the part of the presumed successors. As I mentioned earlier, my wife and I have two children. My son, Sudhansu ("Sam"), is outgoing, makes friends easily, and likes sales and marketing. As a student he did not have much interest in science. With his undergraduate degree in marketing and finance (from St. Louis University), I thought Sam would work for Chemco as the company's "outside" man—hiring, training, and managing the firm's sales force. Sam started working for Chemco as a salesperson and did very well for five or six years. Then he got married, and he and his wife had little interest in working in the family business. He got a sales job with a pharmaceutical company. Later, he received his master's degree in business administration and purchased a small company, Quest Safety Environmental Products, in Indianapolis, Indiana. Under Sam's leadership, Quest has enjoyed significant growth and success. With 2008 sales exceeding $13 million at Quest, Sam is quite happy with what he does, and his mother and I are extremely proud of him. Sam is definitely is not interested in running Chemco.

Our daughter, Sheela, has excellent people skills and, as a student, excelled in science. I thought that after receiving her Bachelor of Science degree in chemical engineering and master's and doctorate in engineering management at the University of Rolla (now Missouri University of Science and Technology), Sheela would take over the manufacturing and plant operation at Chemco. Instead, she developed an interest in teaching. She started at the University of Wisconsin as an assistant professor. Sheela then moved to Indianapolis, where she excelled in teaching and later in academic administration as the director of undergraduate studies, interim dean, and now as the dean of the school of business at the University of Indianapolis, Indiana. She too is doing very well in her chosen career and has a bright future. We are extremely proud of her, too. But, like her older brother, she is not interested in running our company.

My wife and I had a very good succession plan, but it failed because neither of our children wanted to run their parents' business. If your succession plan has better prospects than ours, consider the following:

1. Give yourself plenty of time to plan.

Some entrepreneurs expect to keep working as long as they can. Others look forward to retiring while they are still young, healthy, and energetic to pursue other interests. In either case, you should have a plan for your business when you are not there to make day-to-day decisions. Even if you are planning to continue working indefinitely, it is better for you and your business to have a succession plan in writing to be put in place in case of sudden incapacitation or death.

2. Know the current value of your company.

No matter who inherits or buys your business, it is paramount that you get an accurate evaluation of its worth. A fair value must be arrived at so that, if for no other reason, it can withstand the scrutiny of the IRS. What follows are the six general methods of evaluating a business's worth.

    a. Comparison (market value) method
    b. Cost method
    c. Income capitalization method
    d. Income/cash flow method
    e. EBITDA method
    f. Quick value: bizequity.com

Comparison method

In this method, an appraiser compares the sale prices of three or four recent sales of businesses similar in size to yours, computes the average prices of those location and market businesses, and uses the figure to come up with the average of your business. This method is used widely in real estate. Since there are so many variables even in businesses that are the same size, this method gives an approximate value at best and should therefore be compared to evaluations arrived at by other methods.

Cost method

The cost method determines the replacement cost of all the assets of a business, such as equipment, furniture, buildings, intellectual property (patents, trademarks, copyrights, formulas, and recipes of the products), transportation equipment, along with anything and everything it takes to build a business that size. Once again, this is not a perfect method, and its results should be compared to results obtained by other methods.

Income capitalization method

This method provides a more accurate method of evaluation—that is, if accurate data for gross income and operating expenses have been provided. The income capitalization method involves subtracting a business's operating expense from its gross income to arrive at the net profit and then dividing that figure by the capitalization rate to come up with a value for the business.

A shortcoming of this method is that it includes neither the value of the owner's salary and personal expenses nor that of the business's service debts depreciation and goodwill, so it should be compared with values obtained by other methods.

	Current Year	Last Year	Year Before Last
1. Annual Sales	950,000	850,000	750,000
2. Cost of Products Sold	285,000	255,000	225,000
3. Gross Profit	665,000	595,000	525,000
4. Admin and Overhead Costs	617,500	552,500	487,500
5. Net Income from Operation	47,500	42,500	37,500
6. Owners' Salaries	170,000	170,000	170,000
7. Owners' Payroll Taxes	25,500	25,500	25,500
8. Depreciation	10,500	12,000	14,000
9. Profit Sharing and Retirement	20,000	20,000	20,000
Annual Operating Income (Add 5, 6, 7, 8, and 9)	273,000	270,000	267,000
Three Year Average Operating Income	(273,000 + 270,000 + 267,000)/3 = 270,000		
Small Business Multiplier (5 to 8)	270,000 x 5 = 1,350,000		
Value of the Company	$ 1,350,000		

This value assumes that an absentee owner operates this business. If not, then the manager's reasonable salary and expenses have to be deducted before arriving at the value of the company.

EBITDA method

EBITDA—earnings before interest, taxes, depreciation, and amortization—provides an approximate measure of a company's operating cash flow based on data from the company's income statement. In this method, earnings are calculated before the deduction of interest charges, taxes, depreciation, and amortization. Such an earnings measure is of particular value in situations where a company has a large amount of fixed assets that are subject to heavy depreciation charges, such as manufacturing companies or where a company has a large amount of acquired intangible assets on its books, and in both cases these companies are subject to high amortization charges.

In general, EBITDA is a useful evaluating method for companies with a significant amount of debt financing. It is rarely a useful method for a small company with no significant loans. After calculating the EBITDA value, multiply it by anywhere from two to eight, depending on the industry, to get the value of the company. Once again, compare this value with the value obtained by other methods.

Quick value

Log on to bizequity.com and enter your business name, address, and a few other pieces of information about your company on the Web site. If you have been in business for over five years, you will get a value of your business within minutes. This is a good starting value estimate.

While there are several more methods and ways of evaluating businesses available in addition to the ones outlined above, my suggestion is to get the names of a handful of reputable business appraisers or consultants with experience in your industry, interview them in person, check their references, and hire one to evaluate the value of your business. It is an extremely important component for planning an exit strategy, as the appraisal report and evaluation can be a good point for negotiating with family members or outside buyers for the succession or sale of your business.

The value of the typical small business should always be greater than the total value of its hard assets. The important factor here is that an ongoing business must have in place everything necessary for the buyer to continue the operation of the business, including optimal functioning equipment, plentiful inventory, experienced employees, established business practices, a dependable customer base, the right suppliers, active accounts receivable, timely accounts payable (if the buyer agrees to take them), and cash flow. The challenge to a buyer in a situation like this is how to put the proper value on the intangible assets of the business, which is called the business's goodwill. To arrive at the fair value and accurate figure for goodwill, a business appraiser (generally a CPA) should be recruited.

Execution of succession plan

Do you want to keep the company in the family? If you do, who will take it over for you? The question of which person or persons should assume the reins of a company is one of the most sensitive and emotional issues facing owners of closely held companies. Some family members may wish or expect to be actively involved in the business, while others would prefer to get cash out and pursue other interests.

Once you have decided to pass your business to your child or children, your business partner, or a shareholder, and you have determined the value of your business, you must do the following:

I.   Groom your selected successor and share your vision for the future of the business in which you have invested your life's work.

II. Control your emotions. This once-in-a-lifetime process can be very personal and wrenching.

III. Identify what talents and skill sets will be needed to continue to lead the business and help your successor to develop them.

IV. Give your successor enough room to make mistakes and grow in the business. Be a cheerleader and celebrate your successor's successes.

V. Develop a strategy, through estate and financial planning, for the successful and timely transfer of assets.

Executions of exit strategy

Succession planning of a family business can be a sizable emotional and financial decision for an entrepreneur. Developing an exit strategy from the very business an entrepreneur has started, helped grow, and seen become a success can be even harder to bear. The challenge for the outgoing owner is to plan to exit from his business, even as he prepares the business for the future and retains a meaningful role for himself. Some of the difficult emotional challenges involved in exiting a business include the following:

1. Fear of loss of status

Many entrepreneurs fear that without their business, they may lose the prestige and status among their friends, community, and various organizations they are involved in.

2. Lack of alternatives

Some entrepreneurs have been so busy with their own business activities that they have taken no time to develop hobbies, recreational activities, or friendships outside of their business world.

3. Lack of a qualified successor

The entrepreneur has not found a trustworthy, qualified replacement to take over and run the business after his departure. He thinks he owns the business, but in reality, his business owns him. So he is trapped and continues working.

4. *The need for money*

Some entrepreneurs cannot exit from their business because they need the income to maintain the lifestyle to which they have become accustomed.

5. *Fear of death*

Some entrepreneurs equate their retirement with death and fixate on people who died within a few years of their retirement.

Many entrepreneurs start their business with the idea of eventually selling it and becoming wealthy and then retiring and devoting their time and energy to other interests. If that is your goal, consider the following approaches to selling your business for a substantial profit:

A. Taking the business public (IPO: initial public offering)

If your offering is successful, you will raise a substantial sum of money, and you can also protect your personal savings. In an IPO, the public buys the shares of your company. IPOs can be costly since an investment bank must be retained, which generally charges 7 percent of the total offering. If you raise $100 million through an IPO, the investment bank's fee will amount to $7 million. If the offering value is $10 million or less, banking fees may be higher than 7 percent. There are good and bad seasons for IPOs, and a successful IPO is by no means a given. If you like the idea of an IPO, talk to a businessperson who has tried this method or talk to your banker. Big banks have a department for IPOs. There are companies that go public by selling shares on the Internet, and those fees can be lower than 7 percent. Going public can be very attractive. You get an opportunity to sell some or all your shares, even though you may have to wait for some time to do so. This exit strategy has many drawbacks as well, such as working with Wall Street analysts, spending time defending the price of your stock, filing quarterly reports, and getting used to the ups and downs of your company's stock price.

B. Selling the business to your employees (ESOP)

An employee stock ownership plan (ESOP) is a great idea—both for you and for the business you are leaving behind. It is a good plan for you if you want to sell your business and still retain a measure of control over its operation. ESOPs have been around for over four decades, and thousands of privately held companies have ESOPs. A number of accountants, lawyers, consultants, and banks specialize in ESOP transactions, so find an adviser and learn how an ESOP can be done legally and efficiently. Check would-be advisers' references to discover whether he has a successful track record with ESOPs. Once you establish an ESOP, you can start selling a part or all of your shares in your company to the ESOP and start taking cash out of your company account. If you sell at least 30 percent of your shares to the plan, you can defer capital gains taxes, indefinitely in some cases. Check with your accountant. Regardless of how much you sell, you can run the business pretty much the same as you did before. Your employees keep their jobs, and now they are part owners of the company. They have a motivation to stay in the business, work harder, and share in the profit of the business over and above their regular salaries. However, this plan works well only with profitable companies. An ESOP is like a buyout. The ESOP borrows money from a financial institution against the company's future earnings. The institution buys the shares of company. As the debt is paid off, the shares are released to be distributed among the employees according to the terms of the plan. An ESOP is definitely worth your consideration as an exit strategy.

C. Selling the business on the open market

To sell your business on the open market, you must do the following:

a. Clean up your financial statements

Most small and entrepreneurial businesses are run as sole proprietorships, a distinction from public companies, which are required to provide detailed financial statements for shareholders and regulating agencies. Most small-business owners choose to mask their earnings by such means as accelerated depreciation, excessive compensation, and perks for themselves and their families involved in the business. Some cash business owners do not report all their income to avoid taxes. Some of them deliberately undervalue their inventory and thus hide their actual profits from their operation. You should be aware that such deliberate attempts to avoid taxes are not only unethical and illegal but also undermine the value of your business. After all, most buying decisions are based on the past and future earnings of your company. So it is important that you address and strengthen your financial position, document actual profits from your operation, and pay your fair share of taxes for at least three years, if not all the years you have been in business. Since businesses are bought and sold on earnings multiple, this is the right thing to do.

b. Build a forward-looking management team

Most small businesses revolve around the abilities of their owners. They make substantial profit primarily because their owners work long hours and perform jobs that normally are performed by others in the company. For the potential buyer of the company, this is not very attractive. Buyers might fear that once the sale of the business is consummated, the owner will vanish, leaving the buyer hanging high and dry. So it is important for you to build a second-tier management team that can run your business when you are not there. Most buyers want not only a commitment from the owner to stay up to a year after the company is sold but also a competent, capable management team that has enough know-how to operate the business once the owners are gone. This requires hiring dedicated, professional people, delegating responsibility and decision-making authority, and coaching and encouraging the new team to learn the intricacies of your business and to take pleasure and pride in performing their duties.

c. Establish accurate systems and controls

Have an outside consultant and/or your accountant review your data processing systems and financial controls. These should be computerized so that you can produce good, sound, reliable, and quick financial data and reports for the buyers as needed.

d. Organize your business records

It is important that you develop an accurate and complete accounting of all your business records before going to the market to sell your business. These records include, but are not limited to:

- ✓ articles of incorporation and minutes of directors' and shareholders' meetings;
- ✓ tax records: make sure that you are up to date on your tax filings;
- ✓ leases and any and all contracts binding the company; all should be current;
- ✓ documents relating to all bank loans and individual revenue bonds, if any;
- ✓ documents relating to formulas, patents, trademarks, or copyrights;

✓ all documents relating to USADA, OSHA, EPA, and other city, state, and federal agencies;

✓ accurate payroll records;

✓ any agreements signed with your sales representatives, employees, distributors, and franchiser or franchisees should be current.

e. Improve your curb appeal

You will not have a second chance to make your first impression with your business's buyer(s). When you put your house on the market, you make certain to provide positive curb appeal to impress potential buyers. You should inspect and correct any and all unsightly impressions, both outside and inside your plant or office building. Machines and equipment should be cleaned and freshly painted. Invest in new furniture to make your working space attractive and functional. Clean and blacktop your parking lot and brighten up existing or plant new landscaping—fresh flowers and shrubs. While doing all this costs money, the expense will be a pittance compared to the appeal and interest the showroom-new appearance of your business will generate.

f. Find the right business broker

Selling your business by yourself can be a complex and time-consuming process involving legal, tax, accounting, and regulatory issues. There is also the matter of finding a qualified and willing buyer, to say nothing of negotiating and structuring the most advantageous deal for you. Therefore, it is advisable to look for an experienced and qualified business broker to guide you through the transaction and sales process. To find an experienced, competent, and professional business broker, talk to your lawyer, accountant, banker, and friends who have sold their businesses to get the name of several qualified people.

You should interview at least five business brokers to know that they have successful experience selling a business of your type and price range. Then select the one that you feel most comfortable with.

Most business brokers work on a contingency basis, charging a fee between 2 percent and 7 percent on transactions between $1 million to $50 million and up to 10 percent on a transaction below $1 million. The fee is paid upon closing. The sales agreement between the business broker and the business seller is for a period of six months and is generally on an exclusive basis. Once the broker is hired, he should be provided with all requisite data and given complete cooperation to expedite a sale.

g. Know the potential buyer's reasons for purchasing your business

Once the business broker finds an interested buyer and has a confidentiality agreement signed, the buyer will want to meet the business owner and inspect the company facilities and financial statements. This is the best opportunity to show off your facilities and business in a favorable light. Be open and honest and answer all questions in a friendly and courteous manner. One of the major concerns of most business buyers is that there is something wrong with your business, such as a massive defection of your customers or key employee(s) or product obsolescence. You should be sympathetic to this concern and try your best to make the buyer comfortable with the long-term prospects of your business. Answer all questions and provide all information requested honestly and promptly. While the sales process is going on, run your business with the same vigor and long-term view as if no sale were expected because the sale process may fail. Do not take your eyes off running your business in anticipation of the sale. Nothing can hurt your chances of maximizing value more than sharing disappointing operating results in the middle of negotiations.

Another important consideration in addition to running your business at its peak performance is your employees and what they should be told and to whom it should be told. Inform only those employees who need to know about the sale and who can be of help in the process. Once the deal is reached, all employees will know about the buyer. This will go far in making them more secure and comfortable about their future with your company. If the sale process is conducted properly, it can be done without the large majority of the employees ever finding out about it. To ensure all necessary secrecy, conduct plant tours using a cover story and have meetings and phone conversations off-site.

h. Negotiate the sale

You have now found the buyer for your business. That means:

- ✓ the buyer is willing to purchase your business;
- ✓ he has done his due diligence in examining your financial documents and likes what he sees;
- ✓ he (she) has the cash or loan to make a down payment and finance the sale.

Now it is time to negotiate the terms of the sale. Most business sales are complicated transactions and require the help of a CPA or a corporate attorney, preferably one who is familiar with your business operations, or both.

Your buyer probably will employ the services of a CPA, business broker, or both, and an attorney, whose role it is to find holes in your evaluation method, sales projections, profit margin, and the like. This is all fair game in the buying and selling of a business. You should be ready for this and have confidence in the following:

The Sale Price

You will be required to defend the sale price of your business based on:

    a. gross and net profit generated by your business during the last three to five years;

    b. the price of machinery, equipment, supplies, and inventory;

    c. the value of building and land, if owned by the company;

    d. the value of shares of stock owned by you and other shareholders.

I. Compensation for a noncompete agreement for a certain period of time

The asset sale or stock sale

    i. An asset sale is one in which the buyer purchases the assets of the company. Buyers like asset sales because they receive them free of any problems the company might have had in the past (such as lawsuits, environmental problems, or liabilities). Buyers can also take tax benefits by depreciating the assets over the years. In this case, after the sale, the company pays the shareholders a liquidation dividend.

    ii. A stock sale is one in which shareholders sell their shares in the company directly to the buyer. Sellers like a stock sale because it is taxed at the long-term capital gains tax rate, which is generally lower than that of an asset sale, where a large part of the proceeds may be taxed at the seller's ordinary income tax rate. Be prepared for the asset sale because that's what most buyers want, for the reasons stated above.

j. Contingencies

There are certain terms and conditions that must be met before the sale of your business is complete. They are as follows:

i   the amount, interest, and duration of the financing that the buyer will receive from a financial institution;

ii   the amount of earnest money and terms of return of that money if the deal does not go through;

iii the favorable results of due diligence of all the financial records and other documents of the company presented to the buyer;

iv the acceptable transfer of building, equipment, and/or leases;

v   terms and conditions of owner financing, if that occurs;

vi noncompete agreement for a reasonable and agreed-upon length of time.

k. Warranties

In business sales, the seller and the buyer make warranties and representations to each other, which might include the following conditions:

i.   The seller has the full and legal authority to sell the company's assets or stock and is not in default on any contracts and taxes due.

ii. The seller certifies that all the business records are true and complete to the best of the seller's knowledge.

iii. The inventory of goods and products is good and correct.

iv. All permits, licenses, and certifications are current and up to date.

v.   Any and all employment contracts, cash in the business, accounts receivable and payable, and earn-out agreements are as represented.

l. Seller financing

On this point, be flexible and open-minded. There is no formula that determines the exact value of your business. The sale price of your business is what a qualified buyer is willing to pay for it and what you are willing to sell it for. Do not get emotional at this stage. Most small businesses have a better chance of being sold if there is seller (owner) financing available. As a matter of fact, you can get a better price for your business, earn good interest, and pay lower taxes in most cases if you are willing to partially finance the sale. However, make sure you get at least 20 percent cash down, and check the credit standing of the buyer just as a bank would do. In this case, in fact, you are the bank.

m. Closing the sale

Closing is the final step in selling your business. It is time to bring in your lawyer and accountant to seal the deal. The buyer's lawyer and accountant should be present as well. But it is up to the buyer to ultimately sign off on the sale. Make sure you are in full understanding and agreement with the execution documents prior to attending the closing.

At the closing, both parties will read the prepared documents and sign them in front of a notary public so that the final documents are notarized as they are signed. After the signing ceremony, the funds are dispensed and the sale of your business is complete.

At this point, you can finally exhale—and begin to enjoy your life the way you dreamed you would.

D. Bankruptcy

The mortality rate for small businesses is extraordinarily high. It is said that eight out of ten start-ups will not see their fifth anniversary and that only one of ten will celebrate its tenth. There are several reasons for this high casualty rate, including lack of management expertise, lack of capital, and change in market trends and business environment. From 2000 through

2002, private and public companies had record numbers of bankruptcies. A total of 186 public companies with a staggering $368 billion in debt filed for bankruptcy in 2002 alone. According to the trading service bankruptcydata.com, in 2001 that figure was $259 billion.

The carnage included six of the ten biggest bankruptcies ever. Accounting scandals and greedy management caused WorldCom, Conseco, Global Crossings, Adelphia Communications, and Enron to go out of business.

Domino effect

The downfall of so many once-mighty companies has eroded investor confidence around the globe and obliterated untold shareholders' wealth. These huge bankruptcies have since caused a significant blow to the medium and small companies that did business with these titans and depended on them as vendors, suppliers, and landlords. Remember, the larger the bankruptcy, the larger the domino effect. For whatever the reason, if you find yourself in a situation where you and your business owe more than your personal and business assets, do not panic. Stay calm, cool, and collected. Decide whether you need more time to organize your present business and get on your feet or whether it's better to walk out and start all over again without any handicaps or the burden of enormous, debilitating debt.

In 1987, when the real estate laws changed, the total value of all the properties I owned was about $4 million. I owed about 70 to 80 percent of that amount to different financial institutions. My first idea was to sell all the properties for the balance of the loan and take my losses. As mentioned earlier, the harder I tried, the worse it got. Finally, I decided to sink more money into my properties, raise rents, and slowly pay off the loan. That approach worked for me. However, if you feel that you have tried everything, given your best, and still cannot see a way out, do not despair. Business is a risky game; you should look at bankruptcy as the same. Rid yourself of the idea that bankruptcy carries a stigma. Personally, you can go bankrupt once every seven years and start all over with a good credit score. As a corporation, there is no legal limit to how many times you can declare bankruptcy. Good entrepreneurs look at bankruptcy simply as a time when they struck out and need to get back at bat. So do not hesitate to use the bankruptcy laws if you have to. It is better to get out from under a losing game and start all over again with fresh ideas.

If you decide to declare bankruptcy, the first order of business is for you to find a competent attorney who specializes in bankruptcy law. Check the lawyer out thoroughly. Tell him your problems and get an estimate of his fees. If, in his opinion, the only logical step for you to take is to file for bankruptcy, then do so.

Chapter 11

Chapter 11 is a type of bankruptcy that allows your business to retain control of its operations while it reorganizes its debts. Creditors are prevented from pursuing and harassing a company that is in Chapter 11 proceedings. The debtor usually proposes a plan of reorganization to keep his business alive and pay creditors over time. Official Chapter 11 forms are not available from the court, but you can download them from the Internet at uscourts.gov/bkforms/index.html.

If you decided to file for bankruptcy under Chapter 11, file it immediately so that your creditors do not have time to get organized and force you into Chapter 7 bankruptcy. In the Chapter 7, you will not have control over the trustees, whom the court appoints. Your company will be liquidated. Chapter 7 is very expensive, and the only winner usually is the attorney who is handling the case.

A bankruptcy proceeding is a legal matter, and I am not qualified to give you any legal opinion. However, I can give you a general idea of what you can do to protect your assets. After you file for bankruptcy under Chapter 11, you have some time to concentrate on your reorganization plan without being hounded by your creditors. Once you have the opportunity to work out a plan that you really believe in and under which you feel confident that, given time, you will come out of with flying colors, talk to your creditors in a firm and convincing manner, letting them know that this is the only way they will have a chance to get their money back.

Once you are in Chapter 11, go back to your core business, which made you successful in the first place. Cut costs, overhead, staff, and even research and development. Sign all outgoing checks yourself. Learn to read financial statements—both a balance sheet and a profit-and-loss statement—raise your prices, and increase your sales and profit. Talk to your competitors. Ask them what they are doing that you are not doing. Control your inventory by selling old inventory and unused merchandise. Get travel expenses under control. If you believe in your plan, concentrate on executing it to the best of your ability. If you do not believe in your reorganization plan and you are using it to buy time, you will go into total bankruptcy very soon. But give yourself a good try. You may surprise yourself.

Customers/Clients

Be the first to inform your customers and clients about your financial problems lest they learn about them from others. Call them, write them, and let them know that this is a temporary problem. Tell them as a matter of fact, your products and services will be delivered promptly now since you do not have those creditors hounding you. Let everybody know that you are still around and doing business as usual.

Creditors

Do not avoid your creditors, suppliers, and vendors. Let them know that you believe in your plan of action and you will be out of this financial cul-de-sac soon. Ask for their patience and consideration so that they can emerge with a winning hand.

Employees

You should call a meeting of your employees. Show your positive attitude, and let them know that if they cooperate and put forth extra effort during the time of need, their employment will be steady and rewarded. You will be surprised at how your employees will sympathize with you and keep working above and beyond the call of duty.

Chapter 7

If you have given your best effort day and night to save your business and still cannot see yourself digging out from under, you will have little choice but to file for Chapter 7, total bankruptcy.

Chapter 7 is designed as an orderly, court-supervised procedure by which a trustee collects the assets of the debtor's estate, be it an individual or company, reduces them to cash, and makes distributions to creditors. This course of action dissolves your company and removes you from any financial obligations to your creditors. It destroys your credit, but in some cases, you might be able to come out ahead and start over again.

Being forced out of your business will be an emotionally traumatizing experience for you. But don't blame yourself. You have learned a lot from your experience that will contribute to a better future. Take some time to clean up your mental cobwebs and heal your pain. However, you do not want to take a long time. Do one or more of the following to get out of your painful predicament:

1. Start a new business with a fresh idea and new energy. Avoid the mistakes that led you to declare bankruptcy. The second time will be easier because you are experienced.
2. Prepare your résumé and look for new employment. Employers understand the state of the economy and will see your having owned a small business as evidence of leadership skills and an excellent work ethic.
3. If you are old enough to retire and have enough financial resources, like a retirement fund and IRA, which are protected during bankruptcy, go into retirement with a positive frame of mind.

Now enjoy your life and demonstrate appreciation for what you have—a family that loves you and friends who are proud of you.

E. Closing the door and walking out
This move involves paying off all business debts, selling the assets of the business, and closing the doors. Whatever remains goes to the owner. Such an action can occur in two situations:

1. Your business is failing. You have tried every means available to you but cannot see a successful resolution of your problems.
2. Your business has been very successful. You made a good living running it but could not find a successor or buyer.

In either case, you should close your business elegantly and with dignity. Here is what you do:

1. Notify your customers, clients and suppliers, telling them when you will be closing your business.
2. During the closing period, run your business as usual, with full force.
3. Pay all of your bills, make your final payrolls for your employees, and pay all taxes.
4. Contact the various city, county, state, and federal departments, and close your accounts with them so that they do not assess delinquent taxes on you and your now-closed business.

CHAPTER X

What to Do When You Have Everything

According to Hindu scriptures, a person's life is divided into four stages, each with distinct duties and responsibilities. They are as follows:

Stage 1: Brahmacharya
Brahmacharya is the period of a formal education in which a disciplined student devotes his time and energy to specialized knowledge and vocational training, practices self-restraint, and has complete focus on mastering the subject of his choosing. In modern, Western terms, it's equivalent to pursing an education to study, gain knowledge, and prepare for a productive, meaningful life. A good education and preparation at this stage of your life create virtually unlimited opportunity later.

Stage 2: Grihasthya
Grihasthya means "person of the family." This period is a transition from the life of a disciplined student to the life of a

responsible young adult. At this stage, you apply your acquired knowledge and training to earn money, raise a family, take care of your children, and achieve success, wealth, and fame.

Stage 3: Vanaprastha

Vanaprastha refers to a life of detachment and gradual withdrawal from the demands of daily routines. This is the stage when you plan your succession and exit strategy and retirement. You plan for and train someone to take over your daily work routine, or you sell your business. During vanaprastha, you take the time to enjoy the fruits of your hard work while you are still healthy and strong enough to do so.

Stage 4: Sannyasa

Sannyasa means a life without lust and emotions. This is the time to give your attention and money to worthy causes and to teach and help others so that they can learn by your example. Become a volunteer, a teacher, or a counselor. Write books so that you do not die with your music in you.

I feel that these teachings of a thousand years still apply to modern lives and can help you formulate your plans as you grow in years. Instead of dreading old age, you should look forward to it. If planned right, it offers real possibilities for making your retirement years the happiest time of your life. A happy, fulfilling retirement requires advanced planning and preparation in the following areas:

Financial security

You should have a steady source of income. Social Security has removed the fear of poverty but that is all it has done. Even though we hear the news that Social Security will someday go bust, my feeling is it is part of our system, and it will be available to you in some form or another. But if you want to live better than what Social Security will provide, you will have to do something on your own, such as the following:

a. Invest part of your IRA withdrawal, 401(k), or other savings into an *income annuity* that will pay you a guaranteed income as long as you live. You can visit Web sites like immediateannuity.com and get price quotes from several annuity issuers.

b. Plan to pay off your house, or sell it. Buy a smaller house or a condo and pay it off, or move to a comfortable but smaller apartment. You will be happier if you do not have to make a house payment every month.

c. You may not need two cars anymore. Sell one and pay off the other. Have all your household appliances paid off.

d. Buy a supplementary insurance that covers hospital, surgical, and medical costs over and above Medicare.

e. Have enough money in the bank, such as certificates of deposits (CDs), to cover what amounts to six to twelve months of expenses. No one certificate should have a value more than $100,000 because that amount is the maximum insured by the FDIC. Divide your investment so that CDs come due in three-month intervals. If and when you need to cash in a CD, you can do so with little or no penalty.

f. If you can afford to, you should have an account in some brokerage house like Fidelity (fidelity.com), where you can invest part of your money in a money market fund (which is like cash, earning interest, and can be redeemed anytime), an index fund, and bonds for future growth. If you can afford to lose it, you can invest part of your portfolio in quality stocks, which pay dividends. This plan will help you grow your portfolio to keep up with inflation.

g. You can have direct deposits made from your Social Security, retirement, IRA or 401(k) to your checking account every month. Be sure to monitor your monthly bank statement to be sure your deposits exceed your withdrawals.

h. You can have your utility bills, medical bills, and credit card bills paid directly by your bank from your checking account every month.

The idea behind this is that you create a steady stream of income going into your checking account and your bills are paid automatically. You still will have to check your monthly bank statements, but you do not have to worry about this part of your life. In other words, you put the financial part of your life on autopilot.

Enjoyable and pride-building work

Find regular work that is interesting, builds your pride, and keeps you on a daily routine, especially if you have retired from your earlier high-pressure work or business. This type of work keeps your mind and body active, important things to keep in mind as you advance in age.

If you have some hobbies such as golfing, fishing, woodworking, tax work for others, or writing your memoirs, leaving your life's experience on paper so that coming generations can benefit from it, be sure to indulge yourself in it, as these can be healthful pursuits. Would you like to be a volunteer in a hospital, church, temple, or synagogue? All can make use of an interesting, selfless, and pleasant volunteer. If you like to volunteer, visit volunteer.org for a lot of interesting organizations looking for somebody just like you.

Independence

During retirement, you will want a greater degree of independence than was possible before. So associate with people who are positive and enthused about the future rather than those who are down in the dumps most of the time. Stay away from unpleasant and loud people. The person who makes friends is the one who listens to others politely and with interest. Make friends and associate with people you like.

Good health

As you grow older, aches and pains are a fact of life. Once I called on an eighty-year-old man from India who was visiting his son here, and I asked him how he was doing. He answered, "Oh, I am normal." I visited him later the same evening and found he was having severe pain in his leg. I pointed out that he told me a few hours ago that he was normal. He explained that at the age of eighty, these types of aches and pains are "normal." I know a lot of people who are so busy thinking of others and giving them happiness that their own problems seem to be entirely forgotten. There is no question that good health makes the enjoyment of a happy retirement much easier. You will have good health if you follow the advice given below:

1. Perform some physical work and/or regular exercise every day. It does not have to be long—fifteen to thirty minutes is plenty. Whether your preference is swimming, bicycling, walking, playing golf or tennis, working in the garden, or watering plants, do spend some time in physical activity or exercise every day.

2. Have medical checkups at least once a year or at more frequent intervals. Follow the doctor's specific instructions. Take all the medications on time as prescribed.

3. As you grow older, try to avoid situations that might cause worry and tension.

4. Watch your diet. Your body does not need as many calories as it did when you were younger.

5. Rest and take a nap daily if you can. It is good for you. Go to bed at about the same time every night.

6. Think positive thoughts every day. Be thankful for all the good things that have happened in your life and forget about the things that did not go so well for you in the past.

7. Learn to forgive everybody who has given you pain and discomfort in the past. More important, learn to forgive yourself for the mistakes you have made during the different phases of your life. You are not the same person who made those mistakes. Knowing what you know now, you would not make them. So don't punish the wrong person.

8. Think about today and tomorrow, not about yesterday. You cannot change what happened yesterday. The only thing you can do is to learn from it and use that lesson today and tomorrow.

9. Learn to live every day with happiness, energy, and excitement. An old proverb says, Yesterday is a cancelled check and tomorrow is a promissory note. If you live well today, then it makes every yesterday's memories pleasant and every tomorrow an exciting journey. So live every day to the fullest.

Public office

Public institutions such as school districts, fire and ambulance districts, college districts, metropolitan sewer districts, and village, city, and county boards are looking for experienced people to help run them. This service is rewarding and fulfilling. I ran for a position of a trustee of a junior college district. I did not make it but enjoyed campaigning and meeting people. I have been elected as a councilman of my village twice and love working with our mayor and other councilmen. I enjoy my job as the chairman of the village beautification committee.

Even though I have received more than my share of laudatory publicity in newspapers and elsewhere over the years, the attention that makes me the proudest is the three letters I received from some of our nation's most important leaders: Congressman Richard Gephardt, who wrote about displaying an American flag on Capitol Hill on my behalf; President Bill Clinton, who expressed his appreciation for time I spent as a delegate to the White House Conference on Small Business; and President George W. Bush, who sent me a personal, handwritten thank-you note for work I did in support of his election. These letters are proudly displayed in the foyer of Chemco's headquarters.

Love and appreciation

One of the strongest of all human emotions is a hunger and craving to be loved and appreciated. As you grow older, you feel that your power to do many things, which garnered appreciation and love, is beginning to wane. So your hunger and craving grows more and more compelling. Older people need love not pity. You need people, old and young, to enjoy being with them and talking with them. But you do not have the right to expect a full measure of love and appreciation, no matter what you have done for them.

My wife and I have been very fortunate in this regard. A lot of young people, male and female, some single and some married, have come from India to our great country. They are professionals—information technologists, scientists, and physicians. They are smart and full of energy, but initially they were not comfortable in their adopted country. They needed somebody like Sudha and me, who had been in this country longer and were well established. We in turn needed, and still need, young people like them with vigor, charm, and forward-looking views. Such relationships have proven to be a very symbiotic and invigorating experience for Sudha and me.

In 1999, we had moved into a new 11,000-square-foot custom-built house in a posh area of St. Louis. It was the climax of our achievements, and naturally we were very proud and excited about it. Around this time, a married couple named Jiten and Anju Yadav moved to our town. Jiten has a Ph.D. in plant genetics and is a scientist. Anju is an electronic engineer. They looked in the telephone book and found another family with the same surname as theirs. They called and said they would like to meet us. We found out that Anju's father was a mining engineer and worked in our state in India. Anju was educated there as well. When they talked to us, they thought we were younger people and addressed me as "Bhai Sahib," which means brother. We invited them to our home. When they found that we are lot older than they thought, we instantly became their long-lost aunt and uncle. That relationship became stronger and stronger as time passed on. They were like children to us, and we acted like their parents. We met another couple, Michael Sinclair and Shalini Shama, at a dinner party at the home of two of our closest friends, Shanti and Manorama Khinduka. Dr. Shanti Khinduka was the dean of the George Brown School of Social Work at the Washington University in St. Louis, and Shalini was a graduate student in his school. We liked Michael and Shalini and invited them to our home for dinner.

Every weekend Jiten, Anju, Shalini, and sometimes Michael came to our home. They would cook food for us, eat with us, clean all the cooking utensils they used, and left plenty of prepared food for the whole week for us. We never had it so good.

We loved this relationship. Slowly, we invited other couples like Ajitesh Rai, a neurologist, and his wife, Pallavi Sinha, a dentist; Niranjan and Priti Singh, both physicians; Amit Bhagat and his wife, Lauri, owners of Ameritech Solutions, an IT firm; and Jagan and Haritha Kommu, as well as Suresh and Gayatri Merugumala, all IT professionals. Recently, we met Venkat and Savitha Rao, both physicians, and Vishnu Bishnupuri, a scientist, and his wife, Usha. They all have become part of our extended family. In the beginning, most of them used to come to our home once a week. Then, as they had children, we became their children's grandparents. Our friends became involved with childcare, and they would come to our home generally every other week. As their family grew, they got busier, and they would come to our home once a month. Then every one of them bought their own homes. Now they do not come to our home as often, but we get invited to their homes almost every month, sometimes more frequently, on their birthdays, their children's birthdays, and their wedding anniversaries and for other auspicious events. They treat us like their own parents and the favorite grandparents of their children. Some of the children, especially Jiten and Anju's, think that we are their real grandparents, even when their biological grandparents visit them. We feel much honored the way they treat us with such respect. I call it "the attitude of gratitude."

As mentioned earlier, Sudha and I have two children and four grandchildren. Our son, Sudhansu "Sam" and his wife, Vanita, are both MBAs and are owners of Quest Environmental and Safety Products in Indianapolis, Indiana (questsafety.com). They have two daughters, Anisha, seventeen, and Rina, fifteen. Our daughter, Sheela, and her husband, Daniel Klobusnik, also live in Indianapolis. Sheela, who has a Ph.D. in engineering management, is the dean of the school of business at the University of Indianapolis (www.indy.edu). Daniel has an

MBA, stays home, and takes care of their sons, Deven, six, and Sai Krishna, three.

Both of our children are highly educated and very successful in their selected professions, and we are naturally very proud of their achievements. We are extremely attached to our grandsons and try to see them as often as it is possible. Our granddaughters are now young adults and are doing very well in their schools. We are genuinely proud of our nephews— Rahul and Rohit—for what they are doing to build bright and rewarding careers for themselves and for being role models for generations to come.

My family and I feel blessed to live in this country, which offered us the opportunity to build heaven on earth. We love every minute of it. I say, if we are dreaming, please do not wake us up.

Our formula of love and appreciation may or may not work for you. But find your own formula. Stay with the younger generation; they will energize you. Help folks who need your help at church, summer camps, and mentoring associations. Get involved in your local Lions or Optimist clubs, Knights of Columbus, Elks, Moose Lodge, or other service clubs. You will forget your own aches, pains, and worries while helping others.

Travel

Travel in our own country first and enjoy the beauties of the Grand Canyon, Hoover Dam, Niagara Falls, Lake Tahoe, Catalina Island, magnificent Alaska, and many, many other natural wonders that are part of our national patrimony. How about experiencing the glittering lights and shows of Las Vegas; soothing-all-year weather of del Coronado; cultural institutions and shows in New York; Civil War history in Charleston, South Carolina; golfing in Biloxi, Mississippi; or a skiing challenge on the slopes of Golden, Colorado? Find your passion and energize your life by traveling abroad, a learning experience of other cultures, customs, and people. Traveling to the Mayan sites at and around Cancun, the palace of Versailles, the Tower of London or Buckingham Palace, Taj Mahal in my native India, the Great Wall of China, the pyramids in Egypt—any or all may prove to be the experience of a lifetime. By traveling abroad, you not only learn about those countries but also appreciate how beautiful and grand our own country, the United States, is.

Charitable contributions

Donations to any worthwhile causes and organizations are a way to pay it forward. If you will follow or have followed the steps outlined in this book, you will become a wealthy person. The wealth that belongs to you now belonged to someone else before you had it, and will belong to someone else after you are gone. Everybody who has been born will die some day. In the meantime, you are the custodian of that money and wealth. You are very blessed and fortunate. You can make a difference in the lives of others. You have taken care of your own needs and those of your children and grandchildren. That is your first responsibility. If you can now think beyond your immediate kin, you are an angel of virtues. It is time to leave a legacy, something that will continue to spread your life's achievements to the lives of others forever.

When Sudha and I arrived in St. Louis from India and had children, we found that there was no active religious and cultural organization for our children in St. Louis. I decided to become involved in righting this wrong and became chairman of the then-dormant India Association of St. Louis, helping to organize Indian cultural programs and getting other parents and their children involved. The organization grew, and we decided to build a center. I was one of the founding members of the Mahatma Gandhi Center and its chairman and a member of its board of directors for over a decade. We purchased a five-acre lot, raised over $1 million, and built the center, which has been a focal point of Indian cultural and social activities for over twenty-five years. Working to make the center grow from dream to reality was a challenging task, but one I enjoyed doing, and now I am proud to see all the beautiful programs conducted in it.

Recently, I read an article by Jossi Hempel at CNNmoney. com about Sir John Templeton, who died on November 29, 2008, on his ninety-sixth birthday. According to Jossi Hempel, on the eve of World War II, when a nervous nation was selling stocks, Templeton borrowed $10,000 from a friend and bought a share in every stock on both New York exchanges that was worth less than a dollar. Only four of the 104 companies he bought went out of business. After the war, he invested in Japan, and just as everyone else got into the market, he got out. In 1987, when the market crashed, he went on a buying spree. Then in 1992, after selling his Templeton Growth Fund for $440 million to the Franklin Group, he launched a second career in philanthropy. He founded a $1.5 billion endowment to support the scientific pursuit of spirituality, seeking answers to questions like "Does prayer cure illness?" Sir John, as his friends called him, lived in the Bahamas in a small, boxlike house with flaking paint. His modest kitchen had its original 1969 countertops and cabinets. He drove a modest Kia Opirus car and answered his own phone. His $1.5 million Annual Templeton Prize for Progress Toward Research or Discoveries about Spiritual Relations has been awarded to everyone from Mother Teresa to physicist and mathematician Foreman Dyson. Dr. Albert Schweitzer once said, "Do something for somebody every day for which you do not get paid."

The legendary trustees of huge wealth like Bill Gates and Warren Buffett are prime examples of how entrepreneurs can use their success and wealth to make a difference in the lives of people all around the world. Can you follow these examples in your own ways and enjoy the blessings of giving?

The Man in the Mirror

The real test of your success is how you feel about yourself and how proud you are of your own achievements. The following poem, written by Dale Windrow in 1934, describes the essence of my thinking:

> When you get what you want in your struggle for self,
> And the world makes you king for a day,
> Just go to the mirror and look in the glass
> And see what that man has to say.
> For it isn't your father or mother or wife
> Whose judgment upon you must pass,
> The fellow whose verdict counts most in your life
> Is the one staring back from the glass.
> Some people may think you're a straight-shooting chum
> And call you a wonderful guy,
> But the man in the glass says you're only a bum
> If you can't look him straight in the eye.
> He's the fellow to please, never mind all the rest
> For he's with you clear up to the end,
> And you've passed your most dangerous, difficult test
> If the man in the glass is your friend.
> You may fool the whole world down the pathway of years
> And get pats on the back as you pass,
> But your final reward will be heartache and tears
> If you've cheated the man in the glass.

Search for happiness

One of the primary traits that distinguish successful people from the not so successful is their love of activity. They enjoy all forms of activity and invest everything they do with the same driving energy, whether it's running a business, having fun, or keeping themselves young and attractive.

Abraham Lincoln said, "People are just about as happy as they make up their minds to be." Happiness is a state of mind. Nobody or nothing can make you happy or unhappy unless you allow them to do so. Be discreet with those whom you give your permission and power to please or displease you. Remember the only people who can hurt your feelings are those you care about.

Richard Carlson, in his book *You Can Be Happy No Matter What*, writes that happiness is now. It occurs when you allow your mind to rest, when you take your focus off your concerns and problems. He says "Happiness cannot occur when we place its source outside of ourselves." Happiness is an inside game, and you can and should play it well.

In the 1970s, my wife, our two children, and I lived in a two-bedroom apartment at a monthly rental of $90. Every week, I had my 1966 Chevy Impala gas tank filled at the same Standard service station. In those days, there were attendants who pumped gas while the customers stayed in the car. My favorite attendant was Larry, who was always happy, jolly, and friendly. It was a freezing, cold, and gloomy afternoon when I drove in the station. As usual, Larry came running, started pumping gas in my tank, and wiped my car windows while whistling and grinning. With curiosity, I asked him, "Larry, what makes you so happy in weather like this?" Larry replied, "I'm glad you asked. About five years ago, I was in a dark foxhole in South Vietnam. I made a promise to my Lord that if he got me out of that foxhole, I would never complain about anything. For the last five years that I have been out, I have not broken my promise, and I am not about to."

During 2001, when the dot-com bubble burst and the stock market crashed, most of my friends and neighbors lost a large amount of money. I myself lost close to $1 million in the market. My next-door neighbor, Leonard, came and asked me how I felt. I said, "Leonard, I came from India with $15 in my pocket. Anytime I have more than $15, I feel like a success. My definition of success is such that it is very difficult for me to be unhappy." Leonard remembered that conversation for years, and repeated it with reverence eight years later when my wife and I visited him and his wife, Shirley.

Life is a series of highs and lows; it is especially so true when you get older. Anyone can handle the high points. The big moments take care of themselves. It is the valleys and plateaus that you must learn to handle. Joy, fulfillment, and accomplishment come to you when you establish and sustain a positive inner attitude filled with hope, love, and faith.

Always keep in your mind the old Indian prayer: "God, give me the serenity to accept the things I cannot change; the courage to change the things I can; and the wisdom to know the difference."

CONCLUSION

Coming from a humble background in India, I consider it a great blessing to have lived in the United States of America for the last forty-nine years, first as a graduate student, then a chemist, and eventually and most gratifyingly as an entrepreneur. Starting Chemco in 1975 with $5,000 of my own money and watching it grow to become a leading manufacturer and distributor of environmentally safe and user-friendly industrial specialty and maintenance chemicals has been the thrill of my life.

During the course of more than three decades in business, I experimented with many theories of success until I came up with the surefire formula for financial freedom and happiness that you find in this book.

The bounty of information and advice in *The Formula for Financial Freedom* has been collected not only from my own experience but also from the experiences of many other successful entrepreneurs, men and women who have built countless numbers of enterprises, employed hundreds of thousands of people, and helped make the United States the greatest nation on the face of the earth. If you apply the principles, techniques, and many ideas discussed in this book with your best effort, you will literally make your own opportunities, rather than waiting for them to come to you. You will act like a thermostat, setting the temperature to your liking rather than acting like a thermometer just experiencing too hot or too cold temperature and complaining about it. You will have self-confidence to feel like a victor and definitely *not* like a victim.

Your effectiveness in business comes from your effectiveness as a person. To have a business goal worth pursuing implies that you have a life goal worthy of your best effort. If you do not believe your work is meaningful, you are not likely to give your best effort with passion. You become successful in what you are passionate about. In the long run you hit only what you aim at with focus and passion. So find your passion for what you do or will be doing, as explained in this book, and be your best. It is only in being your best at what you do that you can be truly happy. My only hope is that my formula for your financial freedom and happiness has been and will be helpful in being your best and turning your dreams into reality. After you turn your dreams into reality, your confidence will replace the uncertainty of day-to-day living, and you will think beyond your own needs. You will help members of your immediate family and then humanity at large. *You will enjoy the blessings of selfless giving and unconditional love. By paying forward with your knowledge, finance and devotion you will leave this world a better place than you found it.*

Having advanced to the book's conclusion, you will now receive one last piece of advice. To achieve your financial freedom and realize the American dream, you must read this book at least twice cover to cover! Keep it on your desk and refer to it on a regular basis for three and a half months. I urge you to go even further and review them from time to time so that the principles and anecdotes described in this book will be written, indelibly, in your subconscious mind by spaced repetition and will be handy tools available in your toolbox to solve your problems as and when you face them. As you become more and more comfortable and familiar with the ten chapters in *The Formula for Financial Freedom*, practice what they have to offer to the best of your ability. Be patient with your progress, keep working at it, and success and happiness will be yours. If you have any questions or concerns, please visit my personal Web site, www.theformulaforfinancialfreedom.org, and e-mail me your question, comment, or concern. I will reply at my earliest convenience. I intend to stay with you as your guide as long as you need me. I love to hear from you. I want you to succeed and wish you the very best for achieving the true riches of life.

ACKNOWLEDGMENTS

Many people were helpful in making this book possible, some directly and others indirectly. First and foremost, I thank my wife, Sudha, who has lovingly stuck by me the last fifty-two years, most steadfastly through the toughest times. She raised our two young children and managed our growing business while I was on the road continuously, week after week for several years, getting Chemco off the ground. She has been my life partner, a person of fearless determination, sharp business sense, and tireless effort. My success would not have been what it is without her help and support.

I would like to thank my Ph.D. adviser, guide, and mentor, Dr. George B. Garner, for his continued inspiration and support over the years. He is a great human being and I feel fortunate to have known him and worked with him.

My sincere thanks go to my parents and in-laws, all of whom gave me their unconditional love and whose high expectations for me exceeded even my own. Since they are deceased, I always wonder whether I achieved the level of success they wanted for me.

I want to thank the Tuesday group. In addition to the Khindukas, metioned earlier, and us, there are eight other families in this group. They are Surendra and Meena Khokha,

Hiralal and Kanta Tekwani, Surendra and Kiran Khanna, Raj and Rashmi Nakra, Ravi and Ashu Malhotra, Swaran and Shiv Saxena, Uma and Pawan Aggarwal, and Chand and Deepika Vyas. All of us came from the Indian subcontinent in the sixties and have been friends over four decades. We are like a big family and see one another every time we can, which happens almost every other month. Some members of this group used to play cards on Tuesday, and Kiran Khanna named it Tuesday Group. This group has been a source of inspiration and strength for us over the years.

I proudly thank my adopted homeland, the United States of America, for providing me the opportunity to use my talents to the fullest and to build heaven on earth. The feeling of enlightenment that I get every time I use my in-home custom-built hot tub, sauna, steam bath and multifaceted shower heads, I feel grateful for the chance to build a lifelong happiness here.

I want to thank my personal editor, Richard Lowenstein, who worked so diligently and professionally to make this book an attractive and smooth read. My sincere thanks go to Dr. Steven R. Feldman for his invaluable suggestions and editorial comments, and to my friend Uma Aggarwal for going over the whole manuscript and pointing out several errors for correction.

I thank my associate, Kristy Cruz, for typing the whole manuscript accurately, not once but many times throughout the course of its writing, editing, and publishing.

My thanks go also to Tiffany Nelson for organizing the contents of the book as well as typing it.

Lastly, I want to thank the hard working, talented and courteous editorial staff and the supporting team members at Create Space - an Amazon.com Company for putting this book together in a professional manner.

REFERENCES

Allen, George. *Individual Initiative in Business.* Cambridge, MA: Harvard University Press, 1950.

Ash, Mary Kay. *Mary Kay on People Management.* New York: Warner Books, 1984.

Avis, Warren. *Take a Chance to be First.* New York: MacMillan Publishing Co, 1987.

Bettger, Frank. *How I Raised Myself from Failure to Success in Selling.* Englewood Cliffs, NJ: Prentice-Hall, Inc, 1992.

Carlson, Richard. *You Can Be Happy No Matter What.* Novato, CA: New World Library, 1997.

Carnegie, Dale. *How to Win Friends and Influence People.* New York: Simon & Schuster, 1936.

Clark, Scott. *Beating the Odds.* New York: American Management Association, 1991.

Covey, Stephen. The *7 Habits of Highly Effective People.* New York: Simon & Schuster, 1990.

Curtis, Donald. *Your Thoughts Can Change Your Life.* Hollywood, CA: Melvin Powers, 1975.

Danforth, William H. *I Dare You!, Dare You Committee.* St. Louis, MO: Checkerboard Square, 1927.

Davis, Marvin. *Turn-Around.* New York: Contemporary Books, Inc, 1987.

Eisenberg, Ronni and Kate Kelly. *Organize Your Start-Up.* New York: Hyperion, 2001.

Elker, Harv. *Secrets of the Millionaire Mind.* New York: Harper Business, 2005.

Girard, Joe. *How to Sell Yourself.* New York: Warner Books, 1988.

Greene, Gardiner. *How to Start and Manage Your Own Business.* Bergenfield, NJ: New American Library, Inc, 1983.

Harmon, Frederick. *The Executive Odyssey.* New York: John Wiley & Sons, Inc, 1989.

Harper, Stephen. *Starting Your Own Business.* New York: McGraw Hill, Inc, 1989.

Hill, Napoleon. *Think and Grow Rich.* Chicago: Combined Registry Co, 2003.

Hill, Napoleon and Stone, Clement: *Success Through a Positive Mental Attitude.* Englewood Cliffs, NJ: Prentice-Hall, Inc, 2007.

Kehrer, Daniel. *Save Your Business a Bundle.* New York: Simon & Schuster, 1994.

Kiam, Victor. *Going for It.* New York: William Morrow and Company, 1986.

Kishel, Gregory and Patricia Kishel. *How to Start, Run and Stay in Business.* New York: John Wiley & Sons, Inc, 2005.

LeBoeuf, Michael. *Working Smart.* New York: Warner Books, 1993.

Levinson, Jay. *Guerrilla Marketing.* Boston: Houghton Mifflin Co, 2005.

Mackay, Harvey. *Swim with the Sharks Without Being Eaten Alive.* New York: William Morrow & Company, 1988.

Marcus, Bernie and Blank, Arthur. *The Home Depot, Built from Scratch.* New York: Times Business, 2001.

Murphy, Joseph. *Your Infinite Power to be Rich.* West Nyack, NY: Parker Publishing Co.

Nirenberg, Jesse. *Getting Through to People.* Englewood Cliffs, NJ: Prentice-Hall, Inc, 1988.

Peale, Norman Vincent. *The Power of Positive Thinking.* Englewood Cliffs, NJ: Prentice-Hall, Inc, 1996.

Peters, Tom and Waterman Jr, Robert. *In Search of Excellence.* New York: Harper & Row, 1982.

Quick, Thomas. *Understanding People at Work.* New York: Executive Enterprises Publications Co., Inc, 1982.

Ringer, Robert. *Million Dollar Habits.* New York: Fawcett Books, 1990.

Robert, Cavett and Cundiff, Merlyn. *Positive Thinking Through Hamaneering.* Memphis, TN: Humaneering, Inc. 1977.

Stanley, Thomas and Danko, William. *The Millionaire Next Door.* Hoboken, NJ: John Wiley & Sons, Inc, 1988.

Stanley, Thomas. *The Millionaire Mind.* Hoboken, NJ: John Wiley & Sons, Inc, 2000.

Stone, W. Clement. *The Success System that Never Fails.* Englewood Cliffs, NJ: Prentice-Hall, Inc, 1962.

Timmons, Jeffrey: *The Entrepreneur Mind: Winning, Strategies for Starting, Renewing and Harvesting.* New York: McGraw-Hill, 1989.

Trump, Donald.: *Surviving at the Top.* New York: Random House, 1990.

Viscott, David. *Taking Care of Business.* New York: William Morrow & Co, 1985.

Walton, Sam. *Sam Walton—Made in America.* New York: Doubleday, 1993.

Welch, Jack. *Winning.* New York: Harper Business, 2004.

Ziglar, Zig. *Secrets of Closing the Sale.* Old Tappan, NJ: Fleming H. Revell Co, 1984.

Web sites:

http://app1.sba.gov/training/sbafe/

www.biztaxlaw.com

http://business.uschamber.com

www.chemcocorp.com

www.chemcocorp-gsa.com

www.entrepreneur.com

www.google.com

www.sell-the-goods.com

www.toolkit.com—Business Owners' Toolkit

INDEX

AFTERWORD

The Journey of a Million Miles

With $15 in his pocket, Kamal Yadav, a young chemist from India, came to a new land, the United States of America, in 1961. After receiving his doctorate in chemistry in 1966, Dr. Yadav spent the next nine years researching, working on, and perfecting two formulas—one for environmentally safe cleaning chemicals and another for financial freedom. With his newly developed formula and $5,000 of his own money, Dr. Yadav founded Chemco (chemcocorp.com) in 1975. In the more than three decades since, Chemco has become a multimillion-dollar, debt-free corporation and continues its remarkable, fast- growing pace. The U.S. Small Business Administration and the Missouri House of representatives have honored Dr. Yadav as a champion of the free-enterprise system.

Now, in *The Formula for Financial Freedom*, Dr. Yadav shares his formula for success, explains how he turned his $15 into millions, and shows you step by step how you can do the same.

Packed with irreverent anecdotes, *The Formula for Financial Freedom* offers you all the inspiration, motivation and rubber-meets-the-road information aspiring and existing entrepreneurs and small-business owners need to build a successful business or businesses to achieve financial freedom and to realize life's true riches and happiness.

Dr. Yadav lives in a suburb of St. Louis, MO with his wife of 52 years where he has been serving his second term as an elected councilman. Dr. and Mrs. have two children- a son Sam who is president and chief executive officer of Quest Environmental and Safety Products, Inc. (questsafety.com) and a daughter Sheela who is dean of the school of business at the University of Indianapolis (uindy.edu). They are proud grandparents of four grand children. They have been active in several social, religious and charitable organizations and are immensely grateful to their adopted homeland, The United States of America for the opportunity of their lifetime to build heaven on earth.

Made in the USA
Columbia, SC
19 May 2020